Know
the
Night

A Memoir of Survival

in the Small Hours

Maria Mutch

Simon & Schuster
New York London Toronto Sydney New Delhi

Simon & Schuster
1230 Avenue of the Americas
New York, NY 10020

First Simon & Schuster hardcover edition March 2014

SIMON & SCHUSTER and colophon are registered
trademarks of Simon & Schuster, Inc.

For information about special discounts for bulk purchases,
please contact Simon & Schuster Special Sales at 1-866-506-1949
or business@simonandschuster.com.

The Simon & Schuster Speakers Bureau can bring authors
to your live event. For more information or to book an event,
contact the Simon & Schuster Speakers Bureau at 1-866-248-3049
or visit our website at www.simonspeakers.com.

Designed by Nancy Singer
Jacket design by Eric Fuentecilla
Jacket photograph copyright © by Anton Jankovoy/Getty Images

Manufactured in the United States of America

10 9 8 7 6 5 4 3 2 1

Library of Congress Cataloging-in-Publication Data

Mutch, Maria.
   Know the night : a memoir / Maria Mutch. — First Simon & Schuster
hardcover edition.
      pages cm
   1. Mutch, Maria. 2. Mothers and sons—Biography. 3. Down syndrome—
Biography. 4. Insomnia—Biography. 5. Books and reading—Psychological aspects.
I. Title.
   PS3613.U86Z46 2014
   814'.6—dc23
   [B]
   2013008363

ISBN 978-1-4767-0274-2
ISBN 978-1-4767-0276-6 (ebook)

For R, G & S

Night is only one-half of something and yet it contains all things, even light, even a boy who doesn't speak. *There is no sun without shadow and it is essential to know the night*, according to Camus. It seems that knowing has a cost, and we are changed by paying it, though the result is rarely regret. I'm grateful for a truth amid what I've learned: commiseration is a kind of rescue.

✳

Gabriel is vastly different now. He slept little for a period of about two years, and I can say this about it: I slept little also, it was terrible (as Byrd would say, . . . *in the way that things which are also terrible can be beautiful*), and magic happened. This is the story of that period, of the characters who came to call, the ones who helped us through the night, and a number of incidents that seemed to express a parallel, even sympathetic, mysticism; they are as central to the passing of the small hours, and what the small hours had to teach, as the boy himself.

If there's one thing to be said about the night, it's that companions are beneficial. No one should be alone.

Contents

✳

The cell of the secret is white.

—Gaston Bachelard, *The Poetics of Space*

It had been like dying, that sliding down the mountain pass. It had been like the death of someone, irrational, that sliding down the mountain pass and into the region of dread. It was like slipping into fever, or falling down that hole in sleep from which you wake yourself whimpering.

—Annie Dillard, *Total Eclipse*

provisions for Byrd expedition, Antarctica, 1933–35:

6 straitjackets

[the first crossing] a prologue

A night in late July and the ferry that took us to Newfoundland departed North Sydney at midnight. R and I sailed the Cabot Strait, through the wet air of a black night. It was supposed to be a pleasure trip, but we were vagrants crossing the sea in a tangle of bald lighting, children's cries, and the salt-tinged smell of fuel. People slept on coats under stairwells and in nooks, on patches of floor tile, while others claimed vinyl seats with the ferocity of dogs with bones. After R and I settled into our reserved bunks, I shut my eyes and hoped for sleep.

I tumbled briefly into dreams, and an old man met me there. He drove a crooked finger into my abdomen and stirred. When I gasped awake, there was the static of people whispering, the shifting of the boat. I watched a moth exhaust itself on a bulb. I was two months' pregnant.

At 5 a.m., the great heap of Newfoundland swelled in the dark, and the ferry stopped at Port aux Basques, the cars exiting one by one. Elated to see the first light of morning, I nearly forgot the dream. The sun was pressing and by afternoon, we reached the lake in Gros Morne National Park where we set up camp.

After pitching our tent, we sat on a pebble shore and marveled at the view of a crystalline lake against an emerald hill. We were not alone on this slip of beach. Two French children came along, a beautiful brother and sister. They wanted to play with us, tell us their stories, their words streaming as they tumbled over each other. They were the age when their play unconsciously implied the sexual and they would soon understand they couldn't play in this exact way, the brother pinning his sister, but for the moment they were safe and oblivious. I thought how I would love to have children just like them. Their heavily accented English floated and darted around us as they stood together on the pebbles, panting, to tell us how they came up the St. Lawrence in a great ship, and saw porpoises and enormous birds.

But I was unable to relax, to unclench my fingers from the thermos of tea. Fat cumulus clouds coalesced into the shape of a shark. We sat on the lip of a dazzling lake, and a few moments later, I would start to bleed.

R drove me to the closest hospital, which was two hours from our campsite, in the town of Cornerbrook. The maternity ward was full, so the nurse placed me in a room with three other women and instructed me to remain lying down as she drew a beige curtain around my bed. I felt like a full bowl about to tip.

When visiting hours were over, R was forced to retreat, checking into a motel. The darkness and silence of the ward were cut with pools of light and the wails of an elderly woman in the bed next to mine. She cried out for her left leg, now a phantom, and begged for another hit of morphine. Irritated by her suffering, I wondered what was wrong with me, where was my fucking compassion? I shivered, wanting her to be quiet.

I waited three days for the ultrasound machine that would assess whether I was still pregnant. By the time it pressed its leaking eye to my skin and I had bled seas, it found no life at all.

*

Turn back to the lake, its hard beauty. Our tent somewhere behind us and in front of us silvery water and a green mountain. Two French children sidle up and tell us how they traveled the St. Lawrence on a great ship.

II

Pause for a moment on the dark sea and call to mind Robert Falcon Scott's ship, *Terra Nova*, in 1910 making its way to Antarctica from New Zealand, where he had collected nineteen unfortunate ponies, two of which would die before ever reaching the Ice. Water soaked from the top deck into the sleeping berths where the men had rigged chutes to channel the water away from their heads. They flew lines of cobbler's thread off the stern where albatrosses gathered to collect food scraps thrown from the ship. If a wing happened to brush the line just so, the bird would flip and ensnare itself in a sudden loop of the twine, find itself being hauled in for photographing, a dose of ether, skinning, and transformation into a museum specimen. One of the caught birds, a beautiful black albatross, walked the deck and regarded the admiring men with contempt. Perhaps he knew his power as a mistreated omen, knew that some of them would never make it home.

Midnight

*

spells

Begin again.

Orion is hunting, and black holes drink the universe while Gabriel's squeals and bouncing rock the house. He was born three years after my miscarriage in Newfoundland. He is eleven, but it's been years since R and I have heard him speak. In the absence of speech, then: spikes of sound, vortices, a repetitive soul-splitting screech. Not rage or frustration, not right now, but a wild laughing shriek. Speech pulled to its breaking point. Speech eviscerated. It's just after midnight, and I walk the cold hall to his room, pulled by a loop of auditory fire.

When I open his bedroom door, I find him, small and beautiful, standing in the middle of his room. Autism is one of his diagnoses; there are others. He is capable of communicating—he uses picture symbols to let us know what he wants—but at the moment he's lost, so consumed with laughing and shrieking that the sound itself begins to augment. He disappears this way, erects walls of sound around him as he scurries down internal corridors, leaving the shuddering, sirening body in place for his return.

Gabriel, I say to him. *Gabriel*. He looks at me with blue eyes that contain chips of white, like ice in a sea, but he doesn't see me. When he stops screaming, the air is still but seems marked by the sound. The question is there, too, of how we got to this place in the night and how to get back. How to return him to the other boy he is, the one who looks me in the eye and smiles, the one who loves storybooks and hands me another so I'll keep reading, the one who loves music, especially jazz. The boy in the dark is only one version of Gabriel, one aspect of the night. At the moment, it is impossible to catch and hold him, impossible to define him or put boundaries around him so that he's knowable, though I can comb his vital statistics: four feet nine inches tall, ninety pounds, his sun in Gemini, lover of stuffed bears and applesauce, fearful of dogs, oblivious to cats. When he wakes in the morning, he'll be unironically sweet and calm as he receives his oatmeal and buttered toast, his watered-down juice. He'll wear khakis and a tidy polo shirt, and sneakers he'll try to remove before long. A special-needs bus will pull into our driveway and take him to school, and once there, he'll sparkle some more for the teachers and aides whose adoration of him borders on the ferocious. He has a talent for surrounding himself with loving lions.

But that morning is still far away, and the unpacking of night has just begun. There's a picture on his wall of Louis Armstrong on stage, smiling and holding his trumpet, and it's almost hard for me to look at him in the version of night where he's been playing a gig. I've become envious of him because the night I'm in, the one somewhere in 2008, could as easily be the year before or the year before that. The dark hours have become more or less the same, and midnight is simply the place where we start waking, where we've been waking for two years.

Night used to be different. R and I enjoyed oblivious, unbroken sleeps, even as the parents of two young children—Gabriel's little brother was born four years after him—because both boys slept well. Then, at the age of nine, Gabriel broke one of his nights into pieces, and then most nights after that into more, and then more. Now I go to bed knowing that R or I will be lifted out any time before morning by the sound of clapping or humming or shrieking. Finding him coiled in sounds has become normal, or at least familiar, and it has made me wonder, there in the dark, moving the cat from my legs, about the other parents who are up. I picture them shuffling through hallways toward speechless children, the ones vibrating with the sound of the dark. A reversal happens, and the uninterrupted night becomes the curiosity.

The potency of midnight, when anything can happen, is where our waking begins. Now is the change, the start or end of the spell. We're given a paradox: that in the indisputable presence of night is day's origin, a quiet, winking birth so obscured by flooding ink and our dreams that we barely feel the transition. Midnight, and a corner is turned, and what is gorgeous is also sinister, but mostly we are unconscious or bathed in artificial light when it comes.

Thelonious Monk wrote the tune "'Round Midnight," to which someone later added lyrics, though it didn't need any. *I do pretty well 'till after sundown / . . . But it really gets bad 'round midnight.* The thing about Monk, apparently, was that he would just stop speaking for a while, just decide; days without talking, without explanation. Or sometimes he'd be playing and stand up and stop. Just stop.

I don't look anymore for the reason, how a boy goes from reveling in sleep to simply dabbling in it. His waking, more than the shrieking, has seemed unsolvable, and sometimes I have wondered if the fault is mine. Hubris punished, as in fables. I probably took the unbroken night and the sound of words for granted, and considered them, despite knowing better, as inviolate and maybe even commonplace. In the way that a person can appear to possess what happens out of sheer coincidence to be available, I must have thought they were mine.

When I was in my midtwenties and feeling that something was missing, I started wishing for him. Except that the wish was entirely open-ended—I didn't even specify a him or a her—I simply wanted to be pregnant, and I got my wish, becoming pregnant three times before I was able to carry to term. I had gone to art school, but my mind was concerned with writing, not painting. I had been attempting novels since the age of ten. I completed a full draft of one when I was twenty-one, but by the time I was pregnant with Gabriel—and considering the loss of his words, this is prescient—I suffered a seemingly intractable writer's block. R and I had been married for three years at that point, and I had left my job at a bookstore in downtown Toronto in an anxiety-soaked attempt to keep the pregnancy and to write. I did the latter unsuccessfully, though not for lack of trying; one memorable seven-hour period in front of my computer culminated in a single word on the screen: *jesus*. And I did the former with all the determination I had, as if life can be willed, gritted into being.

Overseeing the first half of my pregnancy with Gabriel was a fertility specialist whose methods for staving off miscarriage involved, among other arcana, the taking of progesterone, a ban on coffee, and no sex. Imagine carrying a raw egg on a spoon, and you have the effect. Imagine the metaphysical equivalent of threads and veils and thumbtacks. But being pregnant with Gabriel was also like being a radio receiver, and I became especially sensitive to my body and knew that I was pregnant before taking a home test, and further that something unusual was happening. When I was five weeks' pregnant, there was a heated point on the left side of my abdomen that felt like an ember hit with air. I curled fetally on the bed for hours on an autumn evening as the tiny pulse of alarm grew, until it was almost midnight and R took me to the emergency room.

We didn't wait long for my examination. I had brought a book with me, imagining that somehow I'd be able to focus on it. The attending doctor, looking to the chair where I'd placed my jacket and the book *Memories, Dreams, Reflections*, by Carl Jung, said, *Whose is that?* While he examined me, he murmured how he admired Jung.

I was admitted, given a bed where nurses hovered and checked and spoke about the results of my blood and urine tests behind the curtain. One nurse said to another, *This woman is really pregnant. Really, really pregnant.* The intimation of excess, of hormones streaming in uncontrolled fountains, was both frightening and reassuring. An ultrasound was scheduled for the morning, and until then time crept. I badly wanted something to drink, but the nurse told me I couldn't drink, or eat, or even brush my teeth, because I'd possibly be operated on due to an ectopic pregnancy. Ectopic, meaning that the embryo had rooted in a fallopian tube instead of the uterus, meaning that the pregnancy could possibly be excised. A sensation, then, like teetering. Pinpricks of waiting, colored chips on the terrazzo floor, the hospital gown's ties like spiders along my spine, and thirst. I waited under buzzing lights until dawn with the faint hope that this pregnancy was not what they thought.

In the morning, an attendant wheeled me through corridors to the dim room where the ultrasound machine stood. Its vision passed coolly through me and glimpsed, there on the uterine wall, a speckling of light and dark. All was well, and the source of the pain was hypothesized to be the spot on the ovary, now a cyst, where the egg that would form Gabriel had made its exit. It had left behind a tiny, fiery explosion. The pain faded, and I shakily dressed in my own clothes again and pressed the gown into a bin. I staggered out with R into the early morning, surprised that I was pregnant; still.

Gabriel wasn't born at night, but on a day in June that was a bright blade. There was the python clench around my abdomen, and the measuring of time in intervals I wanted only to be over. There were the hospital corridors, blank as laundry chutes, and clocks with enormous numerals on the walls. I saw the forms of other mothers moving through the halls wheeling drips, or else propped on beds, and some were talkative or focused, and others seemed not entirely there, as though floating away, like zeppelins. There was R, smiling and coaching me, and the growing feeling within me that all the birthing classes were really just an attempt to give him something to hang on to as I disappeared into the crevasse.

Finally, Gabriel emerged. He arrived lit as lightning, with white-blond hair, and hunched around the hand of the doctor who pulled him free. I can see him perfectly: he arrived as though backing in, facing away. He arrived with his twenty-first chromosomes dangling a third copy.

His Down syndrome surprised me only because I could see then that I'd been right. When I had reached the seventh month of pregnancy, and had been passed from the fertility specialist to my primary-care doctor, I had gone to the library to find books on parenting the typical baby I was expecting. Secretly, I was already concerned. Sometimes the rocking baby inside me would become so still that I would lie down and inwardly beg him, *please move*. So an unease had begun to tingle, and when I walked into the library and started to examine the titles, there it was: *Your Down Syndrome Child*. The spine of the book didn't say *The Down Syndrome Child* or *Children with Down Syndrome*, but *Your*. Mine. The book was old, having been published decades earlier, and full of misinformation. It sat dust-covered on the shelf, as though waiting for me. *Your*.

The diagnosis is both important and not. It is important in that he arrived signifying difference. His entrance was enough to generate a slow-motion tumult in the room, one that gathered speed when it became apparent that he couldn't breathe. The doctor and nurses withdrew him like a magic trick, a flick of cloth and he was gone to the intensive care unit. But this wasn't the only disappearing act: the doctor, one of three women who shared a practice, and who was the first to hold him, began, without my realizing it, to recede. We never saw her again—not once. But his diagnosis is also insignificant because it is only one of numerous that would follow, like beads on a string. He arrived and he was perfect.

✴

Gabriel shrieks again now while I stand in his room. The shrieks are like cyclones, full of movement, and I'm engulfed by the vibrations. It's amazing to me that his little brother, S, who is seven years old and whose room is at the opposite end of the hall, sleeps through this, always. I open one of Gabriel's favorite storybooks, about a lost dog who eventually goes to live in Manhattan, and try to snag his attention, bring him down from the high pitch of his sounds. The dog charges through a park with a dog warden at his heels, while a little boy and girl pretend he belongs to them. Gabriel laughs, wild-eyed, but not at the book; it's some interior vision that has him. The children bring the dog home and lather him in the tub, then introduce him to his cosmopolitan neighborhood. In the last drawing, he's curled on a cushion and seems to be in a deep sleep. Gabriel bounces, his light brown hair flapping against his forehead.

Speech and language are not the same thing, of course. When he's not caught in this midnight vortex, he's eloquent with gestures and facial expressions; he speaks in a language composed of his smiles, grimaces, foot stamps, a range of calls, coos, and guffaws, the way he stands or plops to the ground. He signals with his body. A thrust elbow, he has taught us, is *no*; a clicking kiss sound rewards us for something we did or said. His headshakes and nods are too similar to be sure of, so he has a small board with the words *yes* and *no* written on them, and he points to the one he means.

In the photo that hangs on the wall, Louis Armstrong is on stage, wearing a tux. He's dangling in his left hand his trumpet and one of his white kerchiefs and shaking the hand of trombone player Trummy Young with the other. Armstrong's face, in profile, is electric; he's smiling enormously, and Young is grinning right back at him. You become aware, looking at them, of the silence where you stand and the din of the concert audience where they are. A few feet away from the photo is another image, an abstracted blue trumpet. Underneath it sits a stereo and an iPod loaded with jazz. Gabriel has a captain's bed with drawers underneath, a blue quilt, and a shelf at the head of the bed that's usually kept clear. His mattress has a waterproof barrier and a cushioned pad on top; fresh bed linens are stacked nearby. Before the captain's bed, when he was a preschooler, he'd had a futon flat on the floor because we'd been afraid he'd tumble from a taller bed, even one with guardrails, and the futon had been dubbed his bachelor pad. His grandfather built a hope chest that sits against one wall. It has a secret compartment, but the compartment's existence, its purpose, is hard to convey to someone who has no secrets and is all secret at the same time, and so it remains empty.

Elsewhere in his room, the indications of suspended time: two bins filled to the top with his small stuffed animals (his *twirlies*), the elephants and rabbits and bears with their paws and ears pinched into pointy twists; another bin filled with balls; a yellow bookshelf filled with picture books, many of them from his infancy; plain plastic shades on the windows colored a retreating beige in the hope that he'll leave them where they are; a closet full of the developmental toys—puzzles and foam blocks and toddler games—from which he has never progressed, and stacks of picture symbols, homemade storybooks, drawings from his schoolmates saying things like *Gabe yur the best!* with sketches in bright marker of saxophones and drums; the detritus of various physical, occupational, and nutritional therapies, and missives from the professionals that have come and gone and come again since his birth: pediatrician, pediatric dentist, neurologist, speech therapist, occupational therapist, pediatric ophthalmologist, physical therapist, developmental therapist, gastroenterologist, and psychiatrist.

In the rest of the house, the signatures of the cyclones that have spun out from him: the unbreakable plastic cups and plates and toddler utensils with fat handles, and here and there the patching jobs to cover the dents in the furniture and the black semicircles on the walls where he has swung picture frames when walking by; toys and books that are held together with tape like little Frankenstein's monsters, and the dried speckles of juice, pudding, and yogurt explosions that have escaped the exhausted washcloth. Everywhere you look, the battered, rejoined scene, walls left with a blank stare, cabinet doors that lean from their hinges in a house that has gone elastic. Everywhere, the evidence of entropy and gravity and the provisional nature of the material world in the hands of a boy who doesn't speak.

Before Gabriel, I believed that night is for forgetting in the morning, for a kind of indifference to reality or at least the outward appearance of it, and if we happen to catch a glimpse of night itself, it's through the veil of electric lights. When Gabriel was three— and shortly before I became pregnant with his little brother—we moved from the outskirts of Toronto to a small town in Rhode Island, where we could see the stars, easily, but even with the astronomical readily available, there was still the sense that seeing and being aware of it for longer than the walk from the car to the door of the house is unusual. Humans can be a little estranged from night, stuffing the dark as we do with fears or streetlamps, and that estrangement included me. Until Gabriel began his Sisyphean rising, and rising.

When he was still a toddler, I took him to a playgroup, where a woman struck up a conversation. She asked me if I belonged to a Down syndrome society.

Except that she didn't say, *Down syndrome society*. What she said was, leaning forward and tilting her head slightly, *Do you belong to a secret society?* And then she stopped, laughing with embarrassment, and corrected herself.

It's okay, I said. *It's okay. I know what you mean.*

But entrance to the society, and its knowledge, has a price. Night is composed of the things we aren't meant to see or know, and evidence of my transgression turns up as crying jags, an inability to abide the simplest logic or remember the most fundamental details. Sleeplessness has been so persistent that I commit the lapses of a bland dementia: the coffee mug ends up in the fridge, the milk in the cupboard. I don't see the time of a medical appointment despite it being marked in capitals on the calendar. One day a stoplight seems perfectly green in my reality and I slide through a startled intersection, just narrowly avoiding a tragedy. This is the hallmark of sleepless living, the almost unconscious flirting with potential disaster, the playing with charms that are really electrical wires or scissors. The amount of sleep I get is too short for adequate dreaming, and I stay close to the surface, where the sleep is delicate and prone to dissolving. During the day, my mind feels stuffed with cotton balls and briars, the brain itself rubbed with sandpaper. And yet, in spite of what feels like mental disintegration, I have moments of lucidity, when my visual cortex seems especially charged. In those moments, the symbolism of objects becomes available; the red apple on the counter, the horse's black eye, the white curls on the ocean mean something. Colors break open in a deluge of prismatic code. Van Gogh wrote, *Colors indeed have something to say for themselves.* And if there was anyone who was acquainted with the night and the shattered mind, it was he.

The shattered mind also tends to dwell in isolation. In the night, I'm alone with Gabriel, cleaved from all the sleepers in the world, even the ones I love most. They turn to shadows and slip away. R and S. My isolation, however, doesn't prevent an understanding:

there are other initiates in the society. I know a man who was hired by exhausted parents to be the night nanny to an autistic boy who would rise from his bed and pinch his sleeping sister; my friend's job was to stand sentry at the bedroom door, guarding the sleep, or the waking, of the boy—guarding the night.

I wonder how many of us are in this darkness—and who would take the census, rapping on our shadowy doors, to count us like coins or diseases? I think the number is larger than some would guess, that we move about unnoticed or unknown or cloaked or secret. We are up, with the doctors and nurses and firefighters, because in the night the child's abrasive response to the usual rhythms becomes an emergency. Or at least an emergence. We are up.

The other initiates can be hard to discern, but I look anyway. When Gabriel and I listen to his jazz albums, I know the musicians are speaking a night language, and it feels like an understanding is being traded back and forth; it feels like empathy.

I've looked in other places, too, for the initiates, and in January 2007, I ordered a book online. It was by Admiral Richard Byrd, the polar explorer and aviator. In 1934, while on his second expedition to Antarctica, he attempted to stay in a hut by himself for six months during the part of the polar year when the sun doesn't rise. He made it through four, though nearly died doing so. The book is called *Alone*.

Even the title seemed commiserating. But Byrd wasn't the first discovery in my search for solace. Initially, I was intrigued by explorers in cold places, either poles or mountains, and the idea of their aloneness, and not loneliness necessarily but singularity. The spaces were captivating, the sheets of ice and snow, and either a never-ending day or a never-ending night seemed both beautiful and difficult. There were ships and men locked in ice in the Arctic, and arcs and curtains being drawn in auroras of rippling color. Or I was intrigued with climbers of Everest, for instance, the ones who don't come back and are grafted by cold for eternity to the side of the mountain, made indelible in a hard rumple of clothes. Imagine the subsequent climbers who find the bodies, which are eerily seated, perhaps, as though waiting. So maybe the idea has to do with waiting, or with being found, or being found too late. The idea has to do with the attempt at exploring a difficult place and with whether or not there is rescue.

After the mountain climbers and Arctic explorers, my attention turned to the Antarctic, which seemed even more of a blank. An intriguing Nothingness, one correlative with the psychic regions where I've been stumbling. A place so abstract it came to us first as an idea, providing semantic balance to the North. There had to be a cold, icy South, asserted Parmenides, and then Aristotle. For a time, Ptolemy led everyone astray by insisting that the South was temperate and populated. But eventually it was found, the existential realm of ice, so potent in its ability to wait that its existence was surmised two thousand years before anyone would actually see it. Someone fantasized Antarctica, and it was true.

A supercontinent once existed that contained the bodies of what would become Antarctica, Australia, Africa, India, and South America, called Gondwana (and there is something about the naming of prehistoric—even theoretical—lands that seems uncanny). Over millions of years, Gondwana split apart. Eventually the piece that was Antarctica, dressed in plant and animal life, made a verdant parade through the oceans. It drifted south, turned away, and, like a boy without words, turned inward. It covered its lush land and its secrets with ice.

Eventually there were the explorers who tapped at the edges of the actual place, and the ones of the early twentieth century, such as Shackleton and Scott and Amundsen, who attempted to go farther in, even reach its center, who were driven to insist on their presence in a place that rebuffed them. Some of them died, some of them didn't. The Ice had a dual nature, being both menacing and meditative, composed at once of gigantic, stable plateaus and also changeable cores. The Antarctic is a conundrum, and I have known some of those.

Finally, there was Byrd, who left the suffocating confines of the men and dogs of his own expedition and went more than a hundred miles away. He took meteorological machines with him to assess the void, take its pulse. Really, though, it would seem he wanted to assess himself, explore the void right there at his center. Either way, his story appealed to me, and it didn't hurt that the book pictured on my computer screen featured his face, rimmed in fur, and he was handsome. So I clicked ADD TO CART. Days later the book arrived and I read *Alone*, and I read it again, and I continue to read it and thumb through it and write in its margins and flag the pages with yellow sticky notes and torture the spine, which has held up remarkably well. The sleepless mind is nothing if not obsessive, and so I open the book again and again until it no longer closes.

✳

There is Byrd in his colossal night, the cold morning amplified by waking. For weeks, he watches the sun hover and stutter along the horizon until it fades entirely for the Antarctic winter, a process he speaks of casually, seemingly with little regret as he's watched it go.

But then a small, slick pain. He writes, *as one might watch a departing lover*. Darkness comes, but so too the red spectacle of a vertical line of four stars, a blaze that turns silver, before he decides it's likely one star refracted three times by ice crystals.

Night is never really blank.

✳

For the first six weeks of his life, Gabriel was silent. His cry was only a grimace, and I remember holding him, being awed by him, and wanting badly to hear his voice, and that when it finally emerged, it was small and wavering. It seemed that the start of his language, and the reality of him in a way, was ushered in, like a Zen meditation with the sound of a gong, by this turning point: his cry.

His words gathered a few at a time, and by the age of a year, he had accumulated about twenty before they began to slip away, the typical ones like *pop* and *up* and *bubble*. The words now are ghosts, and I can't hold them in my mind, the sounds of him speaking. I don't remember his first one, and I have to wonder if the forgetting is intentional, as forgetting often is. First words are spectacles, and seismic. They stop a room. The baby promises a trajectory with that first word: one, and then many more, proof of cognition. *Dada* or *cat* or *cookie* synthesizes to a kind of developmental largesse. All is well, it has begun, you can relax now.

Eventually I kept a journal for recording his words, and they appear, in black marker, arranged in rows, along with his signs. We had anticipated oral-motor difficulties, and so one of the therapists who made regular visits to our house taught me to sign. As Gabriel and I talked each day, I drew in the air, and he eventually imitated. While the sound of his words in my memory is thin, the image of him signing is clear, his hands languorous and purposeful at the same time, a sweep of meaning through the air. *Ball* and *elephant* and *airplane*. *Giraffe* and *help* and *milk*. His gestures were fluid and surprising, almost elegant, and his signing vocabulary grew to eighty words—*more* and *mama* and *book*—until meaning pulsed and flickered around us.

The signs, too, vanished. The disappearance was so exquisitely subtle, so already submerged in silence, that it was a long time before R and I realized what was happening. We were so delighted when he did communicate that it masked that he was turning inward, but in the journal, it became apparent that I was recording a decline. From age two to four, the words and signs, every single one, began to slip away. Clutching after them and writing them down did nothing to stop them. We were introduced to a new kind of space, and it wasn't so much that silence was noticed and accounted for; the silence itself was beguiling and formed around us so gently that we could excuse it. Eventually, as the spaces grew larger and he did speak or sign, he could silence anyone around him. The words, when they swaggered in, became legendary.

One such instance occurred when he was three and a half, and he walked into the bathroom where R and I were getting ready for the day. He stood with his fingertips on the counter's edge and, miming our peppery speech, said with perfect clarity, *fuck*. At age four, he sat at our kitchen table with an untouched bowl of fruit, and R asked him—not expecting an answer, just posing the question because you never know, maybe someday an answer would come—why he hadn't eaten any of it, and he responded, *It sucks.* The stricken silence that followed must have lasted a full two minutes. The last times that he spoke, we were unaware that we wouldn't hear words from him again. He was exact and said, *Bye*, at age six, and a year after that, *All done*.

There are therapies but no particular sorcery for the problem of disappearing words, no way to pull them back. From the moment he was born, it seemed, there was much to be done. I was given to think that his development relied on my ability, together with that of countless therapists in various fields, to promote it, and that we had to overcome the invisible forces afflicting him with repetitions and skillful convincing. It seemed to me that I was supposed to solve the problem.

The appearances and disappearances were accompanied by difference all around: he was almost two before he took his first steps. A physical therapy guru arrived from South America to give a workshop on his method, called MEDEK (translated into English, the acronym means Dynamic Method of Kinetic Stimulation), and those of us attending learned circuslike, improbable things. In a large room with a crowd of parents, the babies and toddlers were skillfully flipped and spun. He made the parents gasp by balancing the babies upright on outstretched hands, in just the way that a child learns to vertically balance a stick. We went home and turned our kitchens into therapy rooms, and under the tutelage of therapists practiced this particular magic. And it was there that it happened, Gabriel the toddler, who had been unable previously to stand alone, balanced perfectly, cleanly, with his little feet on my palms; he grew, absurdly, from my open hands. Within weeks, he took his first steps.

And yet. Words have been impervious to inducements and have

developed the slipperiness of what is most desired. It took years for us to understand that our entreaties would do nothing to bring his words back.

*

I was walking through a building one day recently when I saw a sign admonishing people to be quiet. In fact, there were two copies of the sign, just in case the first went unnoticed: Be Quiet Because *Sounds Carry*. And the phrasing struck me suddenly, the suggestion that the sounds aren't passive, but themselves do the carrying, like passengers hauling suitcases toward a train or rescuers laden with limp bodies from rubble. Even as sounds fly off in a rush, they're burdened.

I've come to view the seizures as thieves of Gabriel's abilities. He was five months old when he started having them, what looked like involuntarily gestures, so apparently delicate that he had them in full view for a week without anyone understanding what they were. One after another, the seizures began in his brain and rippled out to his fingertips, so that he simply lifted his arms up to the ceiling, as many babies do to say they want to be picked up. However, in Gabriel, the gesture came with a vague look of surprise. The propulsive nature of the movement was concealed by his low muscle tone, which is characteristic of Down syndrome, and made the motion seem almost casual. He gestured this way again and again, and I tilted my head at him, *What am I seeing?* The appearance, vaguely, of a marionette. Finally, when he was lying on my chest and began to gesture, I felt something like its trajectory, a burst of electricity. He was a semaphore, signaling. The ripple that began in him surged into me, cued cold panic and a call to the pediatrician.

A few days later, R and I found ourselves holding Gabriel in a lab where he was being prepared for an EEG. We'd kept him awake for much of the night so the testing could be done without sedation. R and I paced the beige room, rocking the baby, waiting for him to drift into a deep sleep so that electrodes could be attached to his scalp. By the time the technician finished placing them, a wire sheath snaked up and back from his head into a quietly whirring machine, one that would transmit data to a windowed room a few feet away. R and I hovered, waiting for the process to begin, the machines to hum and the pens to scratch. Someone in the other room watched the scribbles forming on the moving sheet of paper, seizures in cursive, which generated a murmur from the staff. When the test was finished, and we glimpsed the graphs, we saw the sketch of the electrical storm in his brain, a series of spikes and dips, a kind of organized frenzy.

By the time his seizures began, we had had five months to soak in all the information about Down syndrome we could find. Books and articles had piled up at the bedside and in the living room (and these were something like travel brochures and owner's manuals combined) and I had immersed myself in them. There was a long list of possible physical traits associated with trisomy 21: epicanthal folds around the eyes, thyroid issues, neck-vertebrae instability, heart defects, and on, but not a particularly increased risk of seizure. The seizures seemed to have an etiology all their own, to have arrived from nowhere, or said another way, to have arrived from somewhere else. They were evidence of yet another planet in the system. I remember a terrible chill; I remember standing in the kitchen and my knees buckling. There were no words, it seemed, to hold on to.

The neurologist's office was a building just yards from his house. It was easy to imagine him putting on his bowtie and jacket, and drinking a cup of coffee while looking out the kitchen window toward his office, then heading out across the lawn, in the slant rain, or snow, or past impatiens in early spring, to where he delivered the news to anxious parents, tried to explain the mostly impenetrable human brain and just what, exactly, they'd been able to understand. We sat in the waiting room, surrounded by thirty-year-old décor: vinyl seating with paisley designs in green and blue, wood paneling, a pale orange shag rug, all of it impeccably ordered and dustless. When we were led into the neurologist's office by the receptionist, who was also his wife, we found him tall and white-haired with thick black spectacles. He gave the impression of having seen it all, and that was what we'd wanted to find, if not the doctor ensconced in the 1970s, then at least someone white-haired and wise.

He had reviewed the results from the lab and concluded that Gabriel's seizures were infantile spasms, and as he explained them to us, it seemed that the term "infantile" suggested an ephemerality, containment. He told us, as we sat on straight vinyl chairs with metal arms, that when the disorder went undetected and so untreated for an extended period of months, the prognosis was not as good as when the discovery was more expedient, as in Gabriel's case. There was also an increased risk, later on, of autism. We would have to wait and see. He was cheerful and sanguine, and somehow it worked, this silk thread of optimism, and we held it carefully, respectfully, not wanting to fray, or worse, break it. It was a gift and gave us time. When we realized that the extent of damage from the seizures was actually profound and there was, in fact, an autism diagnosis, a number of years had passed. And there it was. The drift of words, a shift, an alteration.

provisions

Inside of this is parenting's alchemical gist: the love for the child becomes so enormous that it mitigates everything else; what would seem anathema to others becomes—to the parent, at least—more or less the status quo. I remember being tired and prickly with self-doubt but also utterly enamored. I remember the trembling, the worry as I held him, but also that life proceeded, that we learned to adapt. Some of the worries faded and so did the seizures once he was given a medication to quell them. I remember that R and I were content, that we found the workings of Gabriel's brain and child development in general fascinating, and I became close with a group of women (wild and strong and visionary) with children with Down syndrome, who put another pulse of energy in my existence. I was consumed, mostly willingly, by the minute details of Gabriel's progress and what the various therapists who had entered our lives were doing with him. The days were a rotation of people—ones with degrees and skills and experience—coming and going, and I was still unaware that words would come and go, too. Eventually, and at least for a period of months, the pervading sense was one of quiet power, of accomplishment. He was a magnetic baby with a toothless smile that was fleeting but so potent that everyone around him pandered to his humor to get him to grin. He was charismatic and a traffic stopper. A friend admiring his tufted blond hair likened him to a baby duck. He smelled fantastic. He learned to sit unsupported, and eventually to crawl, and to bring a spoon to his mouth. His sleep was deep and restorative and entirely reliable; so reliable that R and I often commented on how lucky we were that he was a champion sleeper, how we could recover from each day. We even said about his sleeping, *Imagine if he didn't. Imagine if we were up at night.*

No, stop.

This is the cart before the horse; there was something else. A sound. Another transmission coming through. We anticipated words; we had no reason not to. But after his seizures and before his words (or: after the first silence and before the second), his original quiet was answered by another chasm when he bawled for long periods. The crying didn't seem so different from many typical babies' except that he was older and able to sustain his tight rage for hours. The pediatrician shrugged and mused that it was probably late colic; mused because there didn't seem to be an alternative, another way of saying bald-faced-human-fury-encapsulated-in-an-infant. No other way of saying, at the time at least, the fury that is sometimes autism, a clash of gods delivered in a small body. At this point, it was years before the term *autism* would be applied to Gabriel, because he was still a baby, because his Down syndrome presented an obscuring feint, and because in the year he was born, autism diagnoses were still rarer than Down syndrome. With so many cloaks, he was simply a baby who cried a great deal.

There was a day in the midst of this, one of weeping and pacing and coming undone. He had cried for hours, his body a tight extension of my own, as though he were a raging violin. I had tried ways of carrying him, or I had laid him down. I bundled him or gave him space. I tried to distract either one of us with food or juice, music or toys. I sang, talked, or fell silent. Dimmed the lights or parted the curtains. Provided fresh air or warm blankets. Or nothing, nothing, just an inward attempt, a prayer, for respite. So the seizures were long gone, but in their place came this scorching sound. A siren that the family cat couldn't, for whatever reason, flee. He was drawn, in spite of himself, toward the sound and the baby. When I placed Gabriel on the sofa, still wailing, the cat, who couldn't successfully hunt a spider, made a lunge at his small, smooth head and left behind some scratches and the impression of a tooth.

So maybe we should have known that something else was afoot, that our trajectory had always been headed in a slightly different direction. But not long after this, the fits of crying subsided. And so: the seizures were gone, and the late colic was gone, and in their place came Gabriel's first words. He began, unmistakably, to talk. The magic was there, the silvery presence of words, fast as fish. And it was impossible not to be beguiled.

The Ice

Under the circle of light from my bedside lamp, I take up Byrd's book:

The silence of this place is as real and solid as sound.

His expedition has been on the Antarctic ice for only two months when he decides to make his senior scientist, Thomas Poulter, his second-in-command and leave his fifty-five men at their base, Little America; he will stay by himself in a hut 123 miles to the south on the Ross Ice Shelf, or what he calls the Ross Ice Barrier. Few people have known about his plans—not even his wife, Marie, back in Boston with their four children, knows about the hut that was constructed in Massachusetts and then dismantled for shipping south, or of his intention to stay in it for six months to record meteorological data. (Later, various factions will assert that what he was really after was more acclaim for doing what had not been done.) When the news is delivered to Marie, and then to the audience that tunes into the weekly CBS radio program,* led by his friend Charles Murphy, for tales of the expedition, there is a stream of telegrams to Little America advising him not to go, but he doesn't get the messages. He is already on his way.

His men shore his hut, which will be called Advance Base, with materials that have crossed oceans and ice. Everything he could need, including *Grey's Anatomy*, a fur flying suit, a phonograph,

---

* American audiences were entertained once a week during Byrd's 1933–35 expedition by a program arranged by CBS correspondent Charles Murphy, who was stationed at Little America. The program was said to be responsible for keeping the Antarctic alive in the public imagination at a time when interest in expeditions was waning; people flocked to the CBS studios after dinner in their tuxedos and evening gowns to listen to twenty-odd minutes of live entertainment and seven of foolishness (Lisle Rose, Explorer). A singing group composed of men on the expedition was called the Knights of the Grey Underwear.

canned figs, and two of his mother's Virginia hams. The Barrier where they cut into ice and snow with saws and shovels to submerge his hut is a crystalline blank in a cold that can lift skin from a body. The Ice implies the infinite, and yet he finds himself in a room of 800 cubic feet with thirteen men, including two who will eventually become crucial for him, Pete Demas and Bud Waite. Some of the men arrived before him, hauling supplies with tractors, and have been constructing what he will come to see, in one of his lighter moods, as something like a child's fort. He thinks this before he knows the force of his enemy. Before he finds his own, particular Antarctic.

When they sleep, the men snore so ferociously he opens the lid of his hut and goes topside to regard the night. Peeks in at three of his men in a tent, and walks to the dogs that are tethered to a line, curled tight as pearls against the drift. The Barrier opens up with the sounds of their collective howls. They are ready to leave him.

He, too, has been impatient for his men to go. On March 28, when it finally happens and they lurch off in groaning tractors that have to be coaxed into movement over the ice, he wants his solitude. The machines are poorly lubricated by oil that coagulates and freezes, causing the men to retreat, and he is unhappy when he hears the tractors making a return. When the men leave for a second, and final, time, he is caught by his emotions and rushes up the ladder to watch the diminishing forms.

The next time he hears Murphy's voice, and that of radio operator John Dyer, the sounds are transmitted by radio wave. The antenna is two hundred feet long, and is supported by four fifteen-foot bamboo poles. Because sending voice communications from his hut would require too much power, he telegraphs with a crude knowledge of Morse code. Part of his first transmission to them reads:

All well.

His plan is to fill each day with data collection from eight instruments, among them thermographs, a barograph, a hygrometer (using a human hair to assess humidity), and a minimum thermometer with a heart of grain alcohol instead of mercury, because mercury freezes. The average temperature is -60° Fahrenheit.

The snow on the ground moves with such momentum that he will soon have to dig another tunnel from his hut to form an escape route, in case his other tunnels are sealed over by the drift. The aptness, then, of the word *drift*: its shifting nature, its shiftiness; a movement that could be leisurely or dangerous, but either way is in the possession of some other force.

Not all snow is the same, or the same kind of white. He writes that Antarctic snow lacks the transparency of ice, but the build-up on the ground is so hard that a shovel is almost useless against it. He has to carve it out with a two-foot handsaw. Once new snow has been hardened to the surface, it gives no sign that it has been walked upon. He calls it *the whitest white you ever saw.*

He discovers that two vital items he brought have gone missing in his hut: his cookbook and his alarm clock. He thinks, then, that waking at the correct time is something he can will himself to do through a natural internal sense of the hour.

But night is elastic, and he consistently gets it wrong. He records that it is his checking of the weather instruments that eventually gives him a rhythm. Two pens of the wind register, corresponding to velocity and direction, translate the air currents from the anemometer pole outside his hut. Other pens scratch out temperature readings, and he stands outside and writes his own observations of clouds, mist, and drift.

He says the barrier ice looks like platinum.

*

He was born in 1888 into a Virginia family that his biographer Lisle Rose writes was *avid to regain lost status*. He was a driven navy man, physically small and handsome, a daredevil who played football and led the gymnastics team at Annapolis. He hadn't yet flown an airplane, but in a premonitory way would hurl his body through the air on the rings. At a practice for an intercollegiate championship, he decided to perform a new maneuver in front of a crowd, which involved relinquishing the rings to create a complex turn in midair before catching them again on the way down. He missed, and when he landed on his feet, his ankle snapped and he fell back (he would break these same bones two more times and eventually surgeons would have to nail them together). He wrote in his book *Exploring with Byrd* that he had been aware of silence as he spun, and I've wondered if perhaps this was what cued the fall, if silence, opening suddenly, had beguiled or distracted him.

When his repeated injuries stalled his naval career, he campaigned to learn to fly, finally getting his chance at Pensacola in 1918. Eventually understanding that aviation would be useful to polar exploration, he wanted to be the first to fly to the North Pole, which attempt in 1926 would end up mired in controversy over whether or not he actually reached it. In 1927, he made a nonstop transatlantic flight to Paris (after Charles Lindbergh), all the while allegedly nursing a fear of flying. He decided next on the South Pole and led his first private expedition to Antarctica from 1928 to 1930, and his second in 1933.

Funding for his first two expeditions to the Ice required him, through political and social finesse, to win over wealthy individuals and corporations (Edsel Ford and John D. Rockefeller among them). And though he was an admired figure, being the recipient of not one but three tickertape parades in his lifetime, his second trip generated hate letters (and also, according to Byrd, twenty thousand potential volunteers) because he was going in the midst of the Depression. Once he was on the Ice and had made the journey to his hut, there was more fallout. Some of his men were unhappy with his decision, which they took to be a kind of abandonment, and surreptitiously criticized his mediocre survival skills and lack of proficiency at Morse code. He got the notion to build a fort and despite the antipathy, he did it anyway.

He chased isolation as if it were something to be prized, as if that's really the territory he wanted to see, while dragging along with him tractor loads of weather instruments, batteries, books, telegraph machines, and those Virginia hams; hauling, essentially, an essence of people without the people themselves. He seemed to want to know how far his idea could go. Even he would admit in *Alone* that he was seeking a certain experience, one that we might conclude involves the spirit or enlightenment or some kind of contemplation, though he would say that first he was there to collect data on the weather.

When he and his men of the second expedition arrived to the Barrier in two ships, the *Bear* and the *Ruppert*, they found the frozen buildings of the original Little America, which he had last seen in 1930. At the time, he and his men had left in a bit of a rush and doubtless were not terribly tidy to begin with, and so in 1933, Byrd found their frozen belongings.

Torn parkas and windproof, unmatched mukluks, dirty under-wear and odds and ends . . .

On a table stood a coffee pot, a piece of roast beef with a fork stuck in it, and half a loaf of bread.

Also the pages of a calendar from 1929 with the days marked off. Someone went into one of the other buildings, found the old telephone, and rang them, so that Byrd would write, *If the Lion of Judah had crawled out from under one of the bunks, we couldn't have been more taken aback.* Somebody else flipped a switch and the lights glowed a little. They found pans on the stove with frozen food in them and coal in the scuttle, so they warmed the food and ate it, finding it to be the same as when they had left three years earlier. This is merely the illusion of permanence, however, a way that the Ice will convey constancy even as it perpetuates change, the way that it will obscure the provisional nature of provisions and calm the human presence that is unsettled by the way that everything of substance will eventually disappear.

Gabriel, I say to him after I've been lured back to his room by his sounds. *Gabriel.* He scrunches his eyes at me as he's shrieking, as if he's trying to bring me into focus, but I still don't think he sees me. Not really. He bounces, waving his hands back and forth by his sides, vibrating the wood floor. I imagine the reverberations through each of the rooms, the joists of the house accustomed to the nightly rumbling. *Gabriel,* and the sound is swallowed by his so that when my lips move, there is nothing but his high-pitched squeal. Gabriel: the name that arrived long before he was born. When I was about six months' pregnant with him, I had a list of names, most of which I've forgotten, that I'd been mulling when the *Gabriel* arrived. The problem with knowing what his name should be was explaining that to R. Perhaps he didn't want to challenge me when I seemed so certain, or maybe he'd already figured his chance would come next time, but either way, he acquiesced. When I became pregnant with Gabriel's little brother, R would be the one to decide his name.

Anyway, Gabriel: the shifting, volatile one. We are both lost at the moment, and there is nothing to do but retreat. I pull his door shut as I go into the hall, walk through the chilly air back to bed. R is warm, and undisturbed by the commotion; he, too, has decided, somewhere in the black of sleep, there is nothing to be done. I shut my eyes and try to find something like solace and the passage back into unconsciousness.

Some people count things; I prefer lists, the most mundane kind, the tallies of things left to be done, the groceries and errands, because they are not really mundane. They're about survival. Not only that, but if the most disconnected ideas (compassion, Walmarts, kumquats) are ordered into a list, there is alignment and a semblance of stability, or a chance at them anyway. I think of the polar explorers. I'm fascinated by the lists of what they took with them (in the 1700s, James Cook's expedition brought fearnought jackets— imagine having one of those) for living, for hunting, for finding their way—and what they ate. Especially what they ate. Like the lists of Gabriel's words, the intention says something, though the idea is to gather things rather than lose them.

I have read over and again Byrd's lists of provisions, what he stores in the snow tunnels that lead out from his hut. They hold, in their ordinary arrangements of ordinary objects, the secrets of preparation and daily rhythms. They say nothing exactly about the impossible weather conditions and the unpredictability and danger of the Ice, and yet they are only about these things, with superstitions and desires thrown in, and the suggestion that the dangers can be mitigated if only a person has certain *stuff* in his possession. When I encounter the lists in the right frame of mind, they are transporting. One of my favorites contains, laid against the crystalline blank of the land Byrd inhabits, the incendiary:

> *350 candles, 10 boxes of meta tablets, 3 flashlights, and 30 batteries, 425 boxes of matches . . .*

along with kerosene and gasoline pressure lanterns, fire bombs, and luckily, a Pyrene fire extinguisher. Add also a five-gallon can stuffed with toilet paper, writing paper, decks of cards, oilcloth, pieces of asbestos, and toothpicks.

The means, Byrd says, of a *secure and profound existence.*

I'm not sure the irony is intended. I can imagine him taking stock of what he's managed to bring with him, illuminated by the suspended flashlight that he says makes his possessions seem bigger. Leaving the house with Gabriel requires similar assessment; it requires lists. And clutching the bag full of diapers, wipes, clothing, juice, snacks, picture symbols, storybooks, the spoon with the fat handle, and the stuffed bear with the green hat, I have felt, for a moment or even two, invincible.

Robert Scott's tragic expedition brought ponies, sled dogs, and three motorized sledges. Also reindeer bags, backgammon, and chess. Playing cards, which they rarely used, and books. Apsley Cherry-Garrard, in his firsthand account, *The Worst Journey in the World*, listed Thackeray, Dickens, Kipling, Browning. Says they should have brought some Ibsen.

Once they had reached the Ice and began living in their hut, Scott's men covered their table with a white oilcloth, and on Sundays, they draped one in dark blue. At dinner, they drank lime juice cut with water that sometimes tasted *suspiciously of penguin*. Out exploring, they came upon Shackleton's preserved tents from his *Nimrod* expedition two years before, and within them Rowntree's cocoa, Bovril, Brand's extract of beef, sheep's tongues, cheese, and biscuits—*all open to the snow and quite good*. Imagine them standing there, the Antarctic sprawl and the suddenness of a manmade structure—everything within it suspended, as if insoluble molecules, essentially unchanged; provisions that someone had collected, after mulling what a body would need in this place, and hauled in, leaving what remained for other explorers stumbling by or for the drift's consuming appetite. Either way, knowing that someday a blank would come.

The ponies, said to be somewhat savage, died one by one.

*

There is more here in the night than a mesh of silence, shrieks, and spaces where words are supposed to be. Gabriel's love of music gives us a different kind of to-do list and an actual language. It's the reason that Louis Armstrong is on his wall. The first time I took him to hear jazz, at the suggestion of a stranger, he was nine years old, and we sat in front of a trio: keyboard, stand-up bass, and drums. He'd heard recorded jazz standards many times by that point when

R and I played them on the stereo: Louis Armstrong, Ella Fitzgerald, Billie Holiday, Duke Ellington, and so on to Miles Davis and John Coltrane. But the listening was, in many ways, cursory because the music was in the background, because it was recorded, because none of us was really paying attention.

Gabriel causes a ripple wherever he goes, and this was no different. We sat at a small café table, perhaps less than fifteen feet from the band, and some of the musicians who were waiting to jam and were seated around us had trumpets and saxophones; one guy had sticks. The keyboard and bass traded solos with the drums, the sound of the trumpets came and went, and something in Gabriel expanded. He shut his eyes tight and started to rock, and it was the first time I'd seen him respond to anything, never mind music, as though it were his. Music, of various kinds, especially kids' tunes from the Wiggles and *Sesame Street*, has always gotten him going, but this was like watching an ascent, like watching him understand calculus. He moved through each piece the band played, rolled with it, and the audience could see, too, what was happening in him. They started responding not only to the musicians but also to the way that Gabriel moved and shouted his approval with short, happy shrieks. They hooted and clapped louder when he shouted, they slapped the tabletops.

That was the first time; there have been many since. The irony of his hearing experience is that his ear canals are tiny and twisted, and that at the age of five, he had temporary hearing loss. The surgeon who discovered its origin revealed that between fluid building up on one side of his eardrum and wax hardening on the other, sound wasn't well conducted. Later on, his vision was complicated by significant farsightedness, causing one of his eyes to turn inward; perhaps a consequence was a greater reliance on his other senses.

Whatever the reason, he found one of the things that makes sense of night, and so sometimes when the dark comes, I put him in the car and we drive across bridges strung with lights, and head for a little, nondescript building on a street between a hospital and a police station. Picture him in a Newport jazz lounge where a group of musicians is going to jam.

The waitress has brought him French fries and when he's finished eating, he turns his attention to the band. The notable elements are always the same: the waitress, his fries, his spot, his chair, his shoes removed so he can fold up his legs. The musicians know him, know he'll rock back and forth at certain points, and that he's been learning to clap. Musicians line the bar, some with saxes and trumpets. The players shuffle, play again, discuss chord changes and solos. Somebody asks the bartender for a shot. People stroll in from the street. The guitarist glances up from making adjustments and greets whoever it is, the musicians decide "Isn't She Lovely" or "C Jam Blues," and Gabriel shuts his eyes tight, rocks back and forth. Commiseration, or surrender. In the coiling of one element with another—the texture of the tenor sax with the mottled floorboards, the luminous trumpet with the rope lights pinned to the wall—the sound is smudged one way, sharpened another. The musicians exert and the lounge speaks back, presses in. The door to the street keeps swinging open and closed, people go in and out, and there is snow and ice at the curb. Someone smells of diesel and wet wool, and somebody else heads for the back where the washroom doors say *us* and *them*. And there is the waitress, too: her bare shoulder. A glass of pinot noir appears at the table for me, and the music turns to strands, all sinews and muscle. Gabriel listens with his body, he is in it, and he shuts his eyes again.

He rocks back and forth in his chair, making a soft, high sound of approval when the sax solo comes. At the break, the guitarist says they'll play "Mercy, Mercy, Mercy," and the girlfriend of the trumpet player claps and shouts *All right*, and Gabriel knows he's in for something.

The thing about mercy is that you have to call it down with a certain élan. The original "Mercy, Mercy, Mercy" was recorded in 1966 by saxist Cannonball Adderley. It's a live recording and as the first chords are being played, Adderley speaks on top of them, expounding on the concept of adversity—because if you're going to plead your case, you might mention the thing that got you there—to a crowd that calls back, whistling and hollering when he pauses.

We don't know exactly how to handle it when it comes up . . . sometimes we don't know just what to do when adversity takes over. He sounds like a preacher, and the crowd is drunk and happy and not at all unsure what to do. They holler some more, clap, and stomp their feet. In the version that's happening in the Newport lounge, the audience is doing the very same thing and Gabriel is right there with them.

The experience of jazz, its immediacy when it's played live, gives him quiescence. In the lounge, and in spite of the rocking, he acquires a kind of stillness, or being, or communion. Recorded jazz, played at home on a stereo, will induce this quality for a time. He'll sit cross-legged on the bed, twirl a small stuffed animal between his fingers, and listen; he'll begin to sway. But sometimes the effect can be ephemeral and fickle, so that you never know how long you have before he stirs again and makes his need to explore a room equal with his need to deconstruct it. The thing of disappearing words and bouncing in the night and pervasive developmental delay is that Gabriel's desire to make himself known, and to know himself, catches the flints in his physical environment, the ordinary objects that to him have disturbed, or flashed, or winked. In this mode, he sweeps clear tabletops and desks, shoves to the floor clattering spoons and unbreakable cups, a magazine that was splayed open, or a newspaper that sheds countless fluttering parts. And once, a new computer that had just been pulled from its box.

His production of chaos is an exploration of the random and yet, right in front of him is also the order that he's just rendered: the polished tabletop. Like Camus' Sisyphus, he has a moment of consciousness and surveys where he is. At this point, Gabriel sometimes smiles; he's just turned a world in his hands. He'll shift back and forth on his feet, savoring the way he's extended himself through his fingertips. I know, or I think I know, why he does this, but his tempests often pulse into the surrounding audience as waves of insecurity and doubt, and so R and I will still ask of him, *Why do you do this, Gabriel? Why?*

On the kitchen floor, then, the remnants of breakfast, the triangles of toast, the casual arrangement of jam along the chair seat, the printed pages R or I had tried to read in a quiet moment. And then this from Camus' *The Myth of Sisyphus*, in the paperback edition I've had since university: *What I touch, what resists me—that is what I understand.*

The urge to touch is notorious for winning out. I had taken Gabriel and S to a grocery store, something I almost never do if I can avoid it. The huge vacant aisles and freezing air. I knew better, that I was outnumbered, and that S, being four and a half years younger than Gabriel and intensely curious, would only add to the tangle of elements. I don't remember what it was that I needed to get, or thought was so important, but it drew us through the aisle where the balsamic vinegar sat, nine types of it, in darkly glinting bottles. Gabriel had suppressed his urges until he couldn't suppress them any longer. He pulled on one bottle and then another, and somehow the first landed intact on the floor, but it was the second that fascinated all of us. It collapsed and exploded at the same time: the dead *thunk* of impact, and the almost musical splintering of glass. I was wearing a skirt, and the vinegar splattered up my legs and looked like blood when it dried. A woman pushing a shopping cart stopped a few feet away. She wanted to tell on us so badly, she was vibrating. And there he was: Sisyphus. Except that I could see that I had taken up his position, that having seen so many disasters like this one, I was also caught in a repetition I couldn't escape. Days later, when I was sitting with my therapist in her office, she asked, *So what did you do?*

While I thought it over, she watched me, waiting. Her office is like a removed world, almost submerged. There's a throw on the sofa and enough pillows to build a fort. Tissue boxes and books on meditation line her shelves, and there's a space heater on the floor that faces the client. When she sits, she puts her small feet on a small stool in front of her chair. She has long, slightly unruly hair and the eyes of a lion, and she's prone to saying things like, *The interventions are small*, and *It's not one or the other, it's both*. She also possesses a knack for timing; there was the day that I walked in to find her standing, holding an open book; she looked at me over her spectacle rims. *Second line in* Hamlet, she said. *Stand and unfold yourself*. She smiled, snapped the book shut.

So she asked me what I did in the grocery store. There is a line in Camus' essay that says it, the description of what Sisyphus does when he is standing at the top of the hill and sees his rock roll to the bottom again: *He goes back down to the plain.* It's a moment of consciousness. More than that, the place that awaits Sisyphus, rock and all, a place at an even deeper level of the underworld than where he now stands, constitutes an expanse. Between that and his acceptance, there is the vaguest hint of freedom.

Back at the grocery store, I had taken the boys quietly to the front of the store to let someone know about the mess. But when my therapist asked me what I did, I had to search for the words. I went back down to the plain. *Submit,* I said. *Utterly.*

provisions

Sometimes I'm overtaken by one of those urges that afflict the tightly strung, the need to order one small piece of my environment, no matter how neglected and hoary. I decide on the space beneath the fridge, the magnetic pole that swallows so much of what Gabriel launches into the air. Removing the front vent, I can see the shroud of dust and cat fur, and the forms of numerous objects. I pull out the clumps: a purple twist-up crayon and a blue one, several chocolate chips, a mauve jellybean, three bite-sized squares of buttered toast, a Lego brick, and a profound assortment of glass shards, from tiny slivers like ice crystals and tears to a hefty chunk in pale green—the exact green that I've seen in certain photographs of icebergs. All the evidence of Gabriel's coming undone, or mine. I can see when I press my cheek to the floor that something else is waiting and I slide my hand in as far as possible to catch the edge and drag it out. I sit there, looking at it, and wipe its surface. It's a plastic ruler, in clear blue, with the words written in black, *shatter resistant*.

The Ice

On the morning of April 5, Byrd has been alone for eight days. About to make his morning observation, he climbs the ladder to the door that he designed to open both inward and outward and finds himself sealed in. Banging against it or hanging his body weight from the trapdoor's handle gives him nothing. Topside, the Barrier expands while he is sealed into a room with a Primus stove, a radio receiver, weather instruments, his mukluks, his books. On the surface, katabatic winds thick with ice crystals roar with unbounded freedom while he pounds at the trapdoor with a two-by-four in a burning closet of anxiety.

Let him keep trying to press himself out of what is fast becoming his coffin. The ice desert sprawls above him in its reductive, obscuring simplicity, concealing a world of secrets, from the intricacies of its crystals to the mountains that are tucked unseen beneath the lid of ice. The ice is so imposing that it squashes the form of the Earth into what has been described as a pear shape. Surrounding him is a presence so powerful it transcends any attempts to believe it inanimate; the lid of ice invites a mind, tricks a mind, *is* a mind.

After twenty minutes of battering, he cracks the lid enough for him to fit through and see that accumulated ice and drift have been the problem. He decides then to construct a new tunnel, leading out from his food stores, with an emergency escape hatch. He has only just arrived, but it has begun to happen: the first ideas of escape, its theory, are beginning to form, settle in.

✳

He cuts the silence with his phonograph and the strange, pulled sounds it makes as it begins to wind down. He tries to wash his dishes in the length of a song, makes a game of it, until the notes and words are distorted, tugged like hardening taffy. The cold creeps into the music and is so pervasive it can burrow into the sounds, freezing them from the inside. Silence again, except the clink of his dishes. He clears his throat. Says nothing, however, as there's no one to listen; he is not even on speaking terms with himself.

He writes in his diary, *My table manners are atrocious.*

✳

He thinks the coming of the polar night is not the spectacular rush some imagine it to be. By mid-April, the dark pushes the sun entirely below the horizon. He goes for a walk on the Barrier and becomes sensitive to the artful arrangement of the aurora and the shine of Venus. There is transformation in the night, a turning point in a grand ritual, and quiet. The potential dangers all around him are as obscured by the silence as the crevasse that opened twenty-two years earlier in 1912 and soundlessly swallowed an explorer (E. S.

Ninnis, who had been traveling close behind Douglas Mawson), sledge dogs and all. What emerges for him now is something that he decides is harmony.

provisions

Not long after I took Gabriel to hear jazz for the first time, I took him to hear an eighteen-piece swing band. They usually played in a black box theater, but that night the theater had been taken over by a party, so a little neighboring café swallowed the band whole. Eighteen pieces filled the space, and the audience had to fit itself in and around the band. Gabriel and I ended up seated next to the barisax player, a guy who, when Gabriel threw his juice cup, handed it back to me, smiling.

I knew that when the band eventually started to play, the sound would be concussive and charged, and it's exactly that fullness that holds Gabriel in its embrace. But the band wasn't playing yet; they were waiting for the stand-up bass player who hadn't arrived.

Gabriel was left then with the encumbrance of waiting. He could not tolerate the way time is malleable and unpredictable. He fell apart because he wanted to hear the music and couldn't understand how to make it begin and possess him. He lashed out at me, swiped his hands through the air with a wild look. I caught his hand each time just before impact and moved it to the side, and prayed for the music. Waiting became for both of us a trick, a magical twist in the plot. But he could only be a witness to it, plead wordlessly for his music.

Weeks later, I learned what had caused the delay. The bass player had put his sheet music on top of his car before driving to the café. He discovered in the café parking lot that he'd gotten there without his music, and when he drove back home to locate it, found it sprawled all over his driveway and lawn. Hundreds of pages of rippling sheet music. I imagined him, staring helplessly at the millions of musical notes stippling the ground at his feet, and many miles away the same tempest was swirling in Gabriel.

1 a.m.

*

desire

PROVISIONS FOR BYRD'S HUT:

Meat	360 lbs.
Vegetables	792 "
Beverages	167 "
Soups	73 "
Fresh canned fruit	176 "
Dried fruit	90 "
Deserts [sic]	~~56~~ 75 "

    Tapioca

    Jello [sic]

    Mince Meat

Staples & Cereals

Tool kit

Trail Equipment

Mending kit

Books—100:

    Philosophy

    Science

    Biography

    Novels

    Medical

Meteorological Instruments:

    Double registering anemometer

    Inside and Outside thermometer

Recording barograph

2 minimum & maximum thermometers

Smoke bombs

The conduit between Gabriel and my waking is always sound. His clapping, his voice, or the disembodied flutterings and bangings. At one point in a film about Antarctica, *Encounters at the End of the World*, by Werner Herzog, biologists sprawl on the Ice and listen to the voices of the seals that are swimming underneath. As I lie in bed listening on some nights, Gabriel's moans and calls have a similar haunting, sustained quality, as if the universe is humming through him. As if he's expressing all of his desires at one time and the sounds have blended into a note that seems uncomplicated by meaning except to the initiated listener. The note is so big I can walk around inside it. I wait for him to take a breath. After he does, the sound continues again, hauling all of his desires with it. Effortless and complete.

But this time the sound is different, having stops and starts and cadence. It's like hearing subway passengers speak through the noise of wheels and doors. It seems as though it's coming from his room, except that it can't be. There is R's breath against my ear, and beyond that, what sounds exactly like talking. An electronic toy malfunctioning, maybe, and the recognition that I'm squinting in the dark in order to hear better. Night is pulling a trick. I sit up with my heart racing: *What is that? Do you hear it? What the hell is that?*

R shifts from his sleep and raises his head, strains to hear. He says it as if it's reasonable. *It's Gabriel . . . He's talking.*

So he is, talking in his sleep. Not speech exactly, but speech if intention counts; the roll and rhythm of sentences. Here is what we've been waiting for, the elusive thing we've been hoping would eventually find us. Desire can be potent enough to make the object of the wish substantial, and the mind, desperate to organize what it hears, will break a code whether or not the code exists.

Maybe he speaks for just a few seconds, but in the night, everything is pliable, especially time. Beyond the warp of furled bed-covers and the slim light of the hall, he seems to go on for minutes. We stare into the dark, waiting. I feel a momentary panic, too, at the way meaning seems to be shooting away from us, scattering. Somehow, a portal has swung wide during sleep, if only briefly, and yet we still can't see into it and learn what he means. Here are the words and we can't understand them. We can't understand *him*.

And then it's over, the torrent stops. The night, the dark, the cool air reassemble. Another sound comes and it's Gabriel laughing, a deep long chuckle. The curtains on the windows glow faintly as my eyes are adjusting. I look at R's form in the bed and can tell that he's smiling. *I think*, he says, *that he's telling a joke.*

Perhaps if he had never spoken in the first place, the desire might be different, less acute. He was a child who spoke and became, somehow, one who didn't. Which said that reliable processes were actually tenuous, that his ordinary need to convey a thought could be obviated by something unseen. He likely remembers little about speaking and signing, but whether or not he does, he's certainly aware that he isn't able to do what everyone around him can. And whether or not he remembers, we do.

I gave him a shower recently and was toweling him off when he tried to tell me something. While looking into my eyes, he made a sound with two distinct syllables, ones it was clear he was trying to shape. A small occurrence to the outsider, but to people familiar with him any sound has significance, coming as it does with the opportunity to interpret. (As Margaret Atwood wrote, using stoplights as an example, . . . *if we didn't interpret, we'd be dead.*) The mind wants so badly to understand, to *get it*, that it will chase meaning relentlessly, pursue it straight through the dark. The listener can't help but stop and wait for more and adjust to a slight flurry: did he just speak? what did he say? moreover, what does he want? In those moments, I think that if I knew what he wanted, I would give it—anything. But the sounds, as soon as they were made, disintegrate.

The mind guts the sound archives but comes up with nothing but a guess; the code falls to the floor.

The second-to-last time that he spoke, he was six years old. *Bye.* He said it when we were visiting his grandparents and I was at the door putting on my coat to go out. He had been standing watching me with our relatives, who were arranged in the living room like actors in a tableau. (I picture, even before it happened, everyone frozen in place.) When a child speaks who hasn't said a word in more than a year, then we are not ourselves. I buttoned my coat as I stood in the foyer and waved to him, *Bye, Gabe—see you in a bit!* He stepped forward, locking eyes with me, and memory slows this frame-by-frame so that I'm ready for it when it comes, except that I wasn't. He said, *Bye*, and waved, casually, with his right hand as if he did this all the time. So simple: *Bye*, a step, a wave. I think it's fair to say that, as hyperbolic as I want to be about it, the effect was atomic: a mushroom cloud and obliterating silence. None of us spoke. A version of Gabriel—the one who speaks—had suddenly made an appearance, and there was paralysis all around because we'd been through this before—the wondering what to do because we didn't want to frighten away this particular Gabriel. I knelt down so he could see that I was looking at him, listening, waiting for more. But nothing more came. There was no stopping then the tears that I wanted to hold back. I kissed him, stood up, and adjusted my coat. *Bye, Gabe*, I said. *See you in a while.*

The very last time that he spoke, R and I were not there to hear it. He was in kindergarten. He was two years older than his classmates, who were five-year-olds, as he'd been kept back, against R's and my wishes, by his preschool teachers (special education often seems to be a push and pull between family desire and institutional theory). The end of the day was gaining momentum, and maybe something about this caught his attention. The teacher was packing up, and as she did, said, *All done.* I have wondered how those words crystallized in him, what synaptic leap occurred in his brain that made the idea *all done* form as pure sound in his mouth one last time. It seems like he picked his moment. So he repeated loudly and with the clarity of the previous visitations, *All done!* I like to imagine what has been described to me, the twenty-five heads turning toward him, the engulfing silence. His classmates had never heard him speak and were under the impression that he never had. Jaws went slack in one enormous, synchronized hesitation before the children let out a roar, began jumping and hollering that Gabriel had spoken. It became the talk of the school day. One of the staff, who was also one of his most passionate teachers, called to tell me, *Oh, you won't believe this but* . . .

But I would. I would believe it, knowing full well that his affliction is really that he's so goddamn succinct. So we waited, as with the other times, hoping that the *All done!* was not a finale but the indication of more, and more.

✳

In his baby pictures he's usually laughing. There are so many images of the very round face with toothless grin—he didn't get his first tooth until he was two—that he appears to have been a jovial baby. But what the photos really attest to is my desire to catch and hold his laughter, which was fleeting. Low muscle tone caused his smiles—electric, stunning—to erupt from a flat expression and then vanish, leaving him deadpan again, the changes quick enough to make those of us around him wonder if the smile had really happened.

There is a photo of him that I took when he was too young to smile and anyway seemed to be shrinking from the environment in which he'd found himself; he was just five days old and staying in the hospital's special care nursery. A nurse named Maggie (the spitfire kind, the tough-love kind, the kind you would want if you were mortally wounded) holds him in a plastic basin as she washes him. A feeding tube trails from his nose and his face, with tightly closed eyes, appears to collapse in her supporting hand; white-blond hair in a tuft shoots from his scalp. It's plain that the trading of the dim, watery world for the overly lit one has been harrowing, that he is being engulfed in a sensory assault so profound that there's nothing to be done but give in to it. Time has gotten it all wrong, he is geriatric, and my eldest sister has already pointed out that he resembles our grandfather. You can sense, then, looking at his image—and this is not so easy to do without feeling that a curtain has been parted and the viewing is illicit—that while frailty pervades him, he is a sorcerer, gathering silence with his pink fingertips, drawing it in like a tide.

*

Several years ago when one of my sisters married, after the ceremony and the partying and the sun went down, she had us all traipse with lanterns through a cemetery that was close to four hundred years old. As we wound around the markers, remarking on the names and wondering about the people, we looked at the numerous stones that were broken, lopsided, or sinking into the earth. Some had been smoothed blank by age, suggesting the persistence of the void no one wanted to mention. Inside the disappearance of Gabriel's words, then, the erasure of *us*.

When he was still very little, when he still said Mama and Papa, an older man, who had meant to be commiserating even as he was minimizing, had said to R and me that at least Gabriel knew us, and I thought, Of course, he knows us! His intelligence was, and still is, much greater and more nuanced than his small vocabulary would allow. But with the exodus of his words, the burden of proof would lay itself more and more in R's and my hands. We would find ourselves having to defend his intelligence, what amounts to character and essence and being, to argue the obvious: that a mind is much more than words. Still, there is something in the ability to say, to name, and more than that, there is something in hearing a child's voice, in bearing witness to the grasping and shaping of language and desires, in detecting the wildly small but gleaming planets of early words and being taken up in their orbits.

Thelonious Monk said, *You know what's the loudest noise in the world, man? The loudest noise in the world is silence.* And so here we are, in the night, in the unstopping resonance of a loss.

When I check on S, he's asleep in his pajamas but lying on top of his covers because he's developed a new, exquisitely felt fear that if he pulls his quilt back, he'll find a bed of snakes. At age seven, he's old enough to know that anything can be turned into a Pandora's Box if approached just so, and he's been experimenting heartily, to the point that now the bed *is* full of snakes. Nevertheless, on top of it, he's in a deep sleep.

He was born when Gabriel was four and a half years old. An easy, robust pregnancy, followed by an easy, robust baby. A labor through the night, and his birth right at dawn, on his due date, on a winter day with a pink and orange sunrise that we all exclaimed over before turning back to the baby that R still swears had his eyes wide open. The nurses brought a heaped tray of pancakes and waffles, and the pediatrician pronounced him *Marvelous!* He had one perfectly shaped elf ear, his left, that would stay that way for two weeks before transforming into the usual kind, and nobody said a thing about that.

He was vibrant, and though he would become a boy so loquacious I would suffer the irony of wanting him to be quiet, he would not say one word—not one—for his first two years. It was as though, arriving in our family, he took a look around and con-

cluded that this is what you do: baffle everyone in near proximity
with your glittering, merry silence. There was a day when I was in
the kitchen with the two of them, S the toddler who said nothing
and his six-year-old brother who also said nothing. They sat side by
side, blinking their round innocence at me, and it was as if we were
having a committee meeting, a consultation. *One of you*, I said, *is
going to have to say something.*

And I don't care which one it is.

As jolly as S was as a baby, around the age of two, and when the
words were just starting to come in a trickle before the sudden rush
of fully formed and intricate sentences (one of his first utterances
was the seven-word, *I don't know where the ball is*), he had a brief
period of tantrums. He entered the kitchen one time like a siren,
full-volume, scoring the air. He'd been playing with toys and was,
figuratively speaking, cracked wide open because his father was eating dinner instead of playing with him. The idea of it was engulfing
him (here I picture an octopus clamped hard over a giant scallop),
he was twisting in a tourniquet of toddler rage so profound, it began
to cut him off. I was seated at the kitchen table and he staggered,
bawling, toward it, like someone in a play who's just been shot, so
that all I could see momentarily, before the tabletop obscured him,
was the crest of his head covered in delicate, almost translucent
strawberry waves. The sound emanating from him seemed ancient,
fermented, something dug up. His roar was communicative—I got
the picture, neatly, that he was wild with perceived neglect. Until
that is, the rage choked him off as he was gasping, his eyes wide,
and the siren was abruptly cut short. He passed out, just like that,
on the ceramic tile, went limp and quiet.

The next moments were a strange mix of knowing that he was fine, that his brain had just saved him by shutting him down, and watching myself frantically nudging him, wondering if this would require CPR and an ambulance. Seconds ticked by while he stayed on his back, unconscious. Finally, he blinked awake, took a moment to peer at us hovering over him, and got to his feet. We clucked and checked and pressed him to make sure he was okay, half thinking *of course he is* and half thinking *o jesus*. He took a few steps, taking in his surroundings, and began again to remember it all. He picked up just about exactly where he'd left off, tuned up his fury, and continued a long wail as he staggered again around the house.

The absence of speech, it seems, begets rage. On the other side is the power of a word to make real. One of S's first words was *mama*. When I initially heard it, I was standing in the kitchen. He was upstairs, calling me. He and I were the only ones home, and he must have been about two and a half, meaning that I'd been a mother for close to seven years. He came down the stairs, looking for me, and called out *Mama?* and *Mama?* again. No doubt, he'd said it before, but the combination of the word with being searched out made me realize that I'd never experienced this particular sensation, being found by one of my children.

I wanted to drag it out and hear the word again, so I stayed perfectly silent in the thrill of hiding; the *Mama* sounded so potent. There was nothing quotidian about it; it was all bigness and importance. I think I'd been waiting for that moment, anticipating a kind of being-ness that I'd been trying to conjure since the first attempts to get pregnant (because procreative desire has, attached to its utility, a B side of mysticism; and so there it is, a waiting to be transformed). Each time he called for me, I became present, and more fragile, until I thought he might be worried, and so I called out, *I'm in here!* I heard his footsteps down the hall and he appeared in the kitchen, *Oh dare you are, Mama!* and, not for the first time, I burst into tears.

So S spoke, and then he spoke eloquently, vividly, and began to wonder out loud if there were any treasure chests hidden in the basement or in a closet somewhere, and he went through a period of telling lame knock-knock jokes and roaring with laughter, but there was still Gabriel and his lack of speech. Desire is so persistent a thing that if Gabriel won't speak in the waking world, then we conjure him speaking in the dreaming one. We shut our eyes, slip under, and there he is, talking. It isn't just R and I who have the dreams but a litany of friends and relatives. Even one of Gabriel's school chums dreamed that a meteor landed and when Gabriel touched it, he was able to speak. And because this is the dream world, sudden reversals make perfect sense, so that when he speaks he doesn't just mumble a few approximations but is clear and elucidating and, really, goes on at length, as if he's spoken all along. When I'm the dreamer, my mind races with what I want to ask him—there's so much to know. I want to take his face in my hands, *Tell me everything*, knowing that in this place there's a good chance he will. In my most recent dream, though, the exchange was succinct. He simply told me that he was cold. And in the dream, simple as that, I got him a blanket.

✳

I have agreed to be a ghost. I walk the night hall and think how damn cold the house is. Nothing like what Admiral Byrd has to contend with, but still: cold. All winter I run outside, and yet still find my skin reacting to the air, reacting to the fact that not so long ago I was curled under the duvet. There's something about our house, too, having been built in the seventies and rattled by Gabriel, that it now feels somewhat porous, like an old bone. Night's chilly, slow-moving molecules are simply decanted into the rooms, unimpeded. Our house has breathed in mice and wolf spiders, a squirrel, a chipmunk, and once, a honeybee colony. The hive was in the chimney, and first the odd bee appeared in the upper floors of the house, and then suddenly great numbers of them all around the laundry. One of the basement lights near the washer and dryer has a dangling pull string, which during the time of the bees became covered in them, and turning the light on or off required considerable care. While we worked out what to do with them (we had hoped, before we knew where the hive was, that its position was accessible, and the hive could be extracted whole by a beekeeper, but it was not the case), I got sort of used to their presence and learned to gently brush them off the clothes in the laundry pile in order to do a wash. Their docility turned something in me, and I found myself grieving when the exterminator drove up in his truck.

I climb into bed and watch R, who is sleeping so deeply, almost professionally; it's obvious he'll rumble this way straight to dawn. He is possibly the wisest person I know and his persistent unconsciousness is proof. It's not so much that he is leaving me to it, as I have claimed this patrol as though I am guardian of it. There is a single-mindedness at work in me that excludes everything but the dark, even sex. We collide in daylight, when the rising or falling sun warms the room sideways, when there is a kind of peace, and not here in night's wreckage. Here, I am trying to hold myself together against what Byrd calls *the loneliness of a futile routine*; he writes that *cold does queer things*. So does night. So does desire.

I desired R the first time I saw him, when I was nineteen and walking with friends in the arts district of Toronto. He was wearing combat boots when he slid by on a skateboard. I don't suppose I extrapolated from there two cats, four pregnancies, two children, and a silver minivan with a crystal heart dangling from the rearview, because it was actually another month or two before we would formally meet and another few years before we would date, another three after that before we would marry; in the meantime we were busy with other people. When we did finally go out, it was just a puff, and again we were taken up by others, but we had the same friends and went to the same parties. When it finally hit, the steady gaze that is R, we kissed by a subway entrance on a busy street and I felt not only like I'd arrived home but that I had found that ingredient vital for love, which can be best described, I think, as conspiracy. And so we conspired.

Now many years later I've wondered if at times the night has made me remote, impossible. He experiences my crying jags and outbursts philosophically, empathetically—he can make me laugh in the middle of them or soften the atmosphere by taking my hands; he's the only person to try to hold me when I rage—he is after all caught in the same vortex. His night is broken, too, if not to the same extent. It's an ancient language, and he's the only other one who knows it. He tries to lure me back from the edges of the void where I spend too much of my time dabbling, or alternatively he joins me. The trouble is, more often than not, he is asleep, and I'm unaccompanied. He has said, *Wake me, just nudge me, and I'll get up*, but I have both resented his ability to sleep through many of the sounds and wanted to protect him from the things I'm seeing. I have wanted, too, the ownership of the odyssey. The night is mine, the dark sea is mine, the boat is mine, the Sirens, monsters, and riches—mine. The space around me can sometimes turn the presence of others into nothingness and I worry that, for periods anyway, I become estranged from people I love, and even from myself.

It had been going on for hours one afternoon, Gabriel's laugh-shriek. He had been jumping and flailing his arms and opening his mouth so wide we had a clear view to the back of his throat. Many of the shrieking episodes have merged into new creatures with seams and connecting points, but it's possible that this was the day that R and I drove him around in the car, aiming for somewhere along the ocean—a usually reliable remedy when we have needed quiet—and it didn't work, so that we were then trapped with the sound, belted in and caged until we could get home. I don't remember how we tried to distract him, what songs we sang, toys we dangled, food we offered. No doubt, we also tried to ignore the sound, going about straightening the house, folding laundry, preparing meals. I do remember that at one point S was upstairs in his room with the door shut, still young enough to nap and enjoying one of his fabulously deep ones, the kind he was so expert in, well schooled as he is in the art of tuning out his brother. So one of us was comatose and the rest were performing the enslavements to which we'd grown accustomed. Except that this day was different; it was more taut. We put Gabriel in his room and closed the door, isolating him as if he weren't isolated enough already. Somehow, the force of his shrieking and jumping were barely contained by his room, as if the walls, floor, and ceiling didn't exist. Even downstairs on the main floor, it was as if we were pressed up against him, our sore ears close to his face.

R, who is normally so calm and slow to anger, bounded up the stairs and into Gabriel's room, yelling for him to STOP PLEASE STOP. Gabriel continued and R yelled more, and as I stood in the hall, I could hear the disintegration in R's voice. He was begging. Finally, as Gabriel didn't let up, R understood the futility and joined me in the hall, exhaustedly shutting the door behind him. Gabriel usually trumps everyone else in line for my compassion, but not this time. I thought, See what you've turned your father into? Even as I knew that none of this has ever been Gabriel's choice. And I thought, too, about why we were so alone, why no one seemed to be helping us, though much of the answer to that lies in the way we have kept the dark sea, the boat, and the Sirens to ourselves.

There was another incident around that time, except in this one the person being pulled apart was me, and it was R who was calm, like someone who knew just what to do. Perhaps this is how we manage, take turns at being dismantled, and it was my turn to wonder how a noise like that could possibly emanate from a child and for such a sustained period. It was apparent that Gabriel needed saving and neither R nor I knew how. He was in his room, screaming and laugh-shrieking his brains out, and I stood in the hall, unable to help him in any way and unable to move. Parent-hood delivers with it an assumption of strength, knowing what to do, how to rescue. How not to hate him. How to reach in and find a boy, and yet the knowledge wasn't there. Just paralysis, guilt, a breaking heart.

R took my hands and led me into the bedroom, our bedroom, and shut the door. He kept his eyes locked on mine as he guided me to the bed, and I thought, Now? Are you kidding me? And then the next thought, as I stared back at him—Why not? If we could not rescue Gabriel, we could find each other, and I wanted to be found, made real. Back in university, when we were just beginning, R received his master's in a branch of mechanical engineering called finite element analysis. I understand virtually nothing about it, but the name sticks and I'll use it here for my purpose, to describe what needs to be done when there are whiteout conditions. Sometimes the edges of the void can be felt for, grasped, and it is then that the void ceases to exist or nearly so. Bring in Camus again, *What I touch, what resists me, that is what I understand.*

provisions

His desire for something like a toy or a drink was the very thing we used to lure him out from behind his walls. Gabriel learned to use the Picture Exchange Communication System (PECS), which was developed for people with speech and language problems. Through workshops, I learned how to use the program so I could implement it at home, and then his staff at school learned as well. He was taught to assemble pictures of the things he wanted on plastic strips, forming *I-want* statements. *I want pretzels, I want a drink, I want cheese, I want a show.* A child using the method learns to make requests first by using a single picture, then constructing sentences. One level involves commenting: *I see a blue car; I hear music; I feel angry.*

The upper levels involve a nuance of desire, however, that remains elusive to Gabriel—he doesn't feel the need, maybe, to communicate he saw a blue car rather than a red one—and he's unable, so far, to comment (or perhaps, in the way of astute politicians, prefers not to). But he is a master of I-want, able to extend unexpected significance to a plastic strip with pictures. In the process of learning the method, he was made to seek out his target, the person who would answer his desire, and present them with the strip. Now he'll travel through the house to deliver his message, sometimes throwing the strip to the ground in a huff if we're occupied. I was in the basement when I heard something thwack on the concrete floor beside me: *I want a sandwich.* I looked up to see him standing at the top of the stairs, expectant and shifting from foot to foot. Like any kid, he was too lazy to bother coming down. There are moments like these when I wonder about the minuteness of communicating, the ability of the tiniest movement or expression to convey, and how he must want to be funny or sardonic or ironic. I picked up the plastic strip and suddenly realized what else he intended. *Gabe!* I started to laugh, *I get it—you yelled!*

But in the simplicity of the *I-want* strip: the longing for embellishment. It's easy, seeing how expressive he is with his face and gestures, to imagine how deeply he must want to do what everyone else does: pull the loose threads in a sentence and unravel limitless asides, create the unspoken territories outside of our words. We say blue and yellow, and green hovers there unsaid but as palpable.

There was S, too, expanding his creative influence through provocations and mutterings: the day he stood at the top of the stairs, with his eyes shut tight, yelling *I can't see! I can't see!*, or deadpanning to his father, *I have some bad news. I'm going to annoy you for the rest of the day.* He invented a *fromagus*, a creature whose provenance we've never been able to determine but of which Gabriel appears to be an example (*You are being a fromagus!*), and called a bit of white paper he saw on the ground *lightning*. One day, watching me help Gabriel in the bathroom, he informed me, *I can't stand the meaning of pooh anymore.* On another, he woke up to find that I had dismantled the blanket fort he had constructed the day before.

What did you learn here? I heard him say to himself quietly.

Always guard your fort.

IMPORTANT THINGS, AS LISTED BY S AT AGE SIX:

musics (sic)

monsters

tape

wires

bathrooms

dart

spiked ball

dart (again)

food

The Ice

I go downstairs without turning the lights on, past Gabriel's room where he's now snoring, and down the stairs. I turn on my computer and watch its weirdly secret glow as it boots, the way it seems in the dark like an opening door. But my tendency is to drift aimlessly to the news headlines, the tragedies that are lit and magnified, even glossy. So after several minutes, I shut the thing off again and the blank screen returns with an audible click. Mostly when I can't sleep, I read *Alone*. I want to find the fort, locate Byrd in the void. Pin us both down.

To open his book is to find the hut palpably configured; it seems like it's always been there. I imagine a box of smells in what is reportedly—if far from the edges of the continent and animal life—an aroma-less place, the scent of the hut's fresh beams, the data machines and the alcohol used to keep their ink flowing, soup, seal meat, and the smell of Byrd himself. I imagine the repeated expansion and shrinking of the hut—as if it's breathing—as it warms and cools, how skin can be easily sliced by the proliferating sharp edges, how the sky lights have turned from bright indigo to black to ice-covered, how the Antarctic licks noisily at the hut like it's trying to remove a tick. How wanting hangs tangibly in the air, and perhaps it's the wanting that energizes the scene for me, because that, really, is the point of intersection between me in 2008 and the man in the hut in 1934. What he wants is to survive, and so do I.

The hut, and my observation of it, is a landmark, as if I can draw lines in the dark and note the coordinates; I have something to lead me back. The enclosed feel of the room with the contrast of the Ice bears some resemblance, if only in a symbolic way, to my childhood forts in the woods behind the Nova Scotia house where I grew up, forts that were highly imaginary in nature. As in, there were downed trees and logs that served as perimeters, and the rest I imagined, rather than built. I played at being a spy, or made mud pies with garnish of pine needles, or used the forts as staging areas for my explorations. The magic of my favorite one was that I could still see the house from it, and yet I was firmly in the woods. I tended not to bring friends there, and my sisters were much older, so these were mostly solitary haunts. I understand Byrd's decision to stay alone in the hut, to have complete ownership and feel utterly enclosed. His original idea was that the hut would contain three men, but he eventually decided that he would be the sole occupant. He understands the nature of this place, the night and the void, and that only he has been invited to this particular spot, these exact co-ordinates. (It is true that, whatever the justifications we may use in selecting our cohorts, we are often compelled to bring some people along with us and leave others firmly behind; we say the knowledge is for us, with the *us* being so narrowly defined it can become a unit of one. I know this because I, too, have fallen victim to this way of thinking, erecting a fence around my piece of the night, even as I say I want companions.) I can see him there, hunched at his machines or stirring his tea or preparing to climb his ladder, as if I could just about touch the fur of his coat, pet the animal that he is becoming. This, too, is a kind of desire, one grown from loneliness now that it is night and we are all laconic.

Mornings, he writes, are difficult. He does not want to get out of bed. The black is now so pervasive, he runs through a series of questions when he wakes, who he is and why he's here, in this place, in a sleeping bag, until the sounds of the wind register and the thermograph remind: order, duty, the little world outside his bunk. Ice has begun to creep from the floor and up the walls. After he forces himself into the cold and dresses, he makes tea so hot it scorches. He emerges from his hut to check the day and notes how thinking of a separate day and night has become inane. As if day still existed, and as if night hasn't sprawled over everything.

✳

Water is even more essential than words, so intrinsic that it's easy prey for compulsion when in short supply, and so Byrd is haunted by his need for it. Using a saw, he cuts small blocks of hardened snow from his escape tunnel, and then heats them in a metal bucket on his stove, noting that two gallons of snow converts to only two quarts of water. It is an irony of his situation that he is nowhere near accessible water and yet dwells in its simulacrum. Aside from his unceasing need, it is the stove that imposes, being the source, he believes, of headache-inducing fumes (later, he will believe the source of the fumes is his generator). But the stove doesn't attract his malice, it's the hapless bucket that does. It is a greedy open mouth in perpetual need of feeding; in lieu of a human being, a presence who wants something from him.

✳

He is out on the surface of the Ice, hovering in an unmarked space he hadn't intended. The problem of the Barrier is that there are no barriers, and without them, the self opens, expands, and keeps going. Nothing to bump against, nothing to stop the self from sailing straight away from the planet into the limitless universe. He had been out for one of his strolls, that was all. The two-foot bamboo sticks he'd wedged in the ground and strung with line so that he could lead himself back to his hut through a storm have vanished. The extra sticks he'd brought with him to jam along his extended route are also gone. Twirling himself around in all directions gives him nothing but the same unmarked view. His world has vanished; he has vanished. The Barrier owns him.

Earlier that night as he gazed at the aurora, he thought how beautiful the serpentine curtain looked. He watched and recorded the way it slid over the stars, obscuring them, and then disappeared, leaving the stars in their place again. Yet even an aurora doesn't prevent the mind from grabbing for the world of people, and so he was imagining that he was home in Boston, strolling Beacon Hill, 9 Brimmer Street somewhere in the background, his wife and his children. His study. He often imagines he's elsewhere and sometimes gives ironic designations to the corners of his hut: one is Malibu and another is Palm Beach. Pins in the map from the known world, an ownership that keeps the ice from claiming everything.

Except that now the aurora is gone, his sticks are gone, his way back is gone.

Panic expands in Byrd as he searches in all directions with the beam of his flashlight. Using the stars to mark his way, he walks in one direction and then back, and then out in another.

When Robert Rauschenberg created his white paintings and wrote about them to art dealer Betty Parsons, he referred to the *plastic fullness of nothing*. I think of this when I picture Byrd swinging around for his markers. Somewhere in the plastic nothing, there is a portal that is his hut, the hut where earlier he's been playing Canfield and losing, and listening to Strauss on his Victrola.

And then there it is: his bamboo sticks and line, the giant needles and thread, appear in his beam and lead him back.

All well.

✳

He puts sugar in his soup and ladles cooked cornmeal onto his table thinking his plate is there. The pervasiveness of the cold has eaten snips from his nose and cheeks, the soles of his boots never thaw, and the surface of a glass of water that he sets down shuts with ice within moments. Headaches plague him, and wedged between days of serenity are waves of pain that command his body. His lungs are sore, and going topside sets him gasping. His enemy, he says, is subtle.

As much as he is racked with pain, he is also racked with desire. Here, there is no one to touch him, and no voices, except for the crackling ones from Little America during the radio schedule. He doesn't even laugh out loud because there is no one to share the joke. He longs for voices in another room, certain smells, the feel of rain, temptation itself. He even misses being insulted.

Back on his first night alone when he discovers that his alarm clock and cookbook are missing, Byrd suddenly shouts, *Great God!* and is startled by his own voice, the way that his solitariness is underlined. The way that communication, if anything, implies other people, and the way that a lack of it suggests their disappearance.

✳

In the biography of Byrd by Rose, I find a photograph that intrigues me because it shows Byrd in his hut. It looks like a self-portrait, but the attribution says it was possibly taken later by one of his men as a reenactment. I stare at the scene, at the man and the ordinary objects that attempt to replicate some other place entirely, the place he had wanted originally to escape. He sits at a table, with a silver fork touched to the edge of his china plate. All around are the things he thought he would need, the ones that began their significance in his lists. In the absence of people to talk to at dinner, he reads to himself as he eats, and so in the image, a book lies open on his lap. More books can be seen piled under the table, almost as though they are holding it up. His hair is longish, combed straight back and bushed out about the neck as he grimly regards his food. The items around him, stacked up on shelves or hanging from nails, are evidence of the human will that has been able to contrive digging a hole in the Antarctic and bringing icons of the known world to fill it. On the table, there is an open package of Salada tea, a silver pitcher, a lantern, a teacup, small tins, and papers; a shelf above holds more tins and jars, and papers are pinned to the wall; hanging behind him is a pair of scissors and a hacksaw. Outside the frame of the picture, what you can't see is the dangerous blank his belongings are meant to mollify. Even amid the isolation he deliberately sought, with his objects as symbols of his lost world, he tries to carry on as if he isn't truly alone.

✳

It's the middle of May and the voice of John Dyer at Little America comes through the radio receiver like cracked pepper, repeating Byrd's call letters,

KFY . . . KFY . . . Can you hear me?

He tells Byrd the odd bit of news from the world, the one of people and countries and stock market crashes, but the significance cannot travel the distance. The words do not console Byrd or alleviate his solitariness and instead seem *almost as meaningless and blurred as they might to a Martian.* Though he can hear their voices over the radiotelephone, he has to communicate back to them by telegraph, which presents its own set of obstacles. The transmitter, sitting in his food tunnel near a ventilating pipe that leads to the surface of the ice, has to be powered by a generator, which in turn has to be warmed beside his stove before he can pour fuel into it and haul it back to the tunnel. In order to start the generator, he has to fit a cord around a flywheel and then yank on it to spin the engine, lawn mower–style, then he heads back to where the telegraph sits on his table to confront the lines of Morse code that he barely understands. If he knows what is going to be discussed, he plans out what he wants to say, writing the letters in vertical columns and then marking down the corresponding dots and dashes; he does this knowing that as soon as Dyer or Murphy or Waite says something unexpected, he won't be able to keep up. Communicating, then, is a burden; it is difficult to say what he means, difficult to find the drive to do so. What he understands now is the creep of ice in his hut and changing the sheet on the barograph. He longs for the sight of trees, the sound of a foghorn. The temperature falls to -65° F, then -72° F, and the ink of the thermograph finally freezes despite being mixed with glycerin. The Barrier stops sending its messages.

He's digging in his Escape Tunnel when the anemometer cups start rattling. Wind on the Barrier has increased, so much so that it travels the ventilator pipe and snuffs the red candle that had been lighting his work. He goes topside to make his observations, and the wind blows out the fire in his stove. A blizzard is working itself up, so he makes a second trip onto the Barrier to check the wind direction. But the ravenous whiteout gulps his vision, his hearing, his reason. He pulls up on his trapdoor, but it doesn't budge. As he tears at it, his mind hurtles through white space and his body is battered. Flailing about, he finds the top of his ventilator pipe. He looks down into it and sees the warmth and definition within that was so recently his.

He remembers a shovel lying somewhere around him in the drift and begins a search. Holding onto the pipe or the edge of his door, he lies flat on the Barrier and kicks out with his legs until finally he hits the shovel. He wedges the long end into the door handle and heaves up until the door springs open.

The storm snarls overhead, and he is depleted but safe in the small dark space of his hut. There is no one to speak to, so he simply thinks it: *How wonderful, how perfectly wonderful.*

2 a.m.

*

soul

PROVISIONS FOR BYRD:

BEVERAGES

Tea	1 case
Cocoa—prepared	1 case
Sanka coffee	1 case
Ovaltine	4 14-oz cans
Torex	1 case
Bovril	12 8-oz jars
Malted Milk	2 cases—chocolate and plain

SPECIALS AND CANDY

Cheese	2 Limburger, 2 Roquefort, 2 Swiss, 2 Old English, 6 American
Swedish Bread–Rye Crisp	5 cases
Black Psylla Seed	5 cans
Predigested glucose	6 cans
Grapefruit juice	1 case
Lemon in sugar	1 case
Hard candy	
Peanuts	6 cans
Popcorn	12 small cans
Gum	3 boxes

Marshmallows	½ box
Saltines	10 cans
Chocolates	3 boxes
Bar Chocolate, Nestles	
Mixed nuts and pretzels	
White psylla	1 can

I have shovels and battering rams of my own. There are three ways for me to reach the safety and light of the symbolic fort. The first is running, as in the practice of going for a run, which I do in the mornings. And which lends itself to metaphor too quickly perhaps—that I am running from something or to it—when in reality the motivation seems to have something to do with present time, with feeling my body and its limits. I run sometimes on a forested trail that curves along a bay. The trail's surface changes from sand to wood mulch to leaves, and in some places, the soil has been pounded hard by feet and horse hooves so tree roots appear to pull up the earth in fistfuls. The ground requires attention and it becomes a kind of study, how to land my feet without twisting an ankle. On a recent run, my mind was pulled between assessing the path ahead and thinking over words and desire—mostly desire—entwining them, pulling them apart, when my foot caught a tree root, hooked it. It was like being thrown to the ground by a giant. I was aware suddenly of torn muscles and scorched skin; I was aware of being slammed into myself, tossed in there with the monsters and gravity and night.

There was a quiet, blinking solace while I sat on the ground and examined the soil mashed into my hands, my right hip, the spray up my legs. The ground beneath me seemed to be smoothing over its attempt to devour me, while the ache on the right side of my body had already begun. I got to my feet, took a few tentative steps, as though testing the ground, whether it would grab me again, and finished my run.

The body's judgment is as good as the mind's, and the body shrinks from annihilation, wrote Camus.

I run sometimes at night, because it's another way of knowing the dark. I've run with groups of people after sundown, but I've also run alone, using a small headlamp to light the way on the bicycle path where there are no streetlamps and the surrounding area is all woods and wetlands. The night has its controversies. Running alone in the dark is something I'm told I'm not supposed to do, but that instruction feels negating to me, as though the only ones entitled to the night are men. It would seem to me that it is the killers and bears that should stay at home. But the returning message is that in the night, you get what you deserve. Step out alone and into it and, well. You're really on your own then.

When Byrd set out for his hut, he had the right idea. The Barrier still had some light, so he could settle in and wait for the dark to gather around him, which is another thing entirely than marching headlong into the black. I tested this theory unintentionally when I went for a run as the sun was going down. As it grew dark, my headlamp lit the path directly in front of me but to the sides were amorphous margins full of possible creatures, too many to count. At first, it wasn't so bad. The problem arose after I'd gone three miles to a point where the path intersects civilization, where there's a road and a streetlamp. I stood under the light for a moment, bathed in contrast, feeling relieved until I turned and saw that the trail to get back appeared to be a black cave. I would have to run straight into it for the same three miles to get back to my car, which I did, as fast as I could. The terror seemed to be fueled more by the suggestive area between what the headlamp illuminated and what it did not than by the black itself. The possibilities added a layer of terror to the terror, so that by the time I reached my car, I was practically incandescent with fear.

I went back on another night, because this seemed like something I needed to dismantle, or get inside of, or defy. But this time, when the sun dipped down and things turned black, instead of turning on my headlamp and igniting those peripheral ghosts, I let my eyes adjust. I ran as if I were invisible and limitless and one with everything I'm afraid of.

✳

The second route home is jazz, because it collects Gabriel and brings him along, effortlessly. Because it can speak to both night and desire.

When jazz musicians would stop by the cathouse (so named because, aside from the jazz cats who came to call, over a hundred felines dwelled there), jazz lover Pannonica de Koenigswarter would ask them if they had three wishes what they would be, and she wrote down their answers. Sonny Rollins said, *To be able to do what I want to do on the horn*, Mary Lou Williams said, *To love God more*, John Coltrane wanted *three times the sexual power I have now*, Anita

O'Day *To be active until I die. You know! Up and at 'em like!*, and Stan Getz wanted justice, truth, and beauty. Bill Evans just wanted a wishing ring so the other two wishes would be unnecessary.

Gabriel and I have been out to hear jazz in various little spots in Rhode Island and Connecticut about two dozen times. Now we're at a lounge in Newport having a listen. I see a guy at the bar glowering with the band's dissonance, with one beer too many. He came into the bar in search of nothing but a drink, and so he soon rolls off his stool like he's on a listing boat, shoves a folded bill across the bar, and gives a broad, disgruntled wave in the direction of the band. He's had enough. If it's about anything, jazz is the body, distracting or obliterating itself with sound. Love like a seizure. Desire and its accoutrements, its gowns and dresses, half-shredded on the floor. And it's not for him.

Gabriel, however, is finding his way. Maybe you really have to want something in order to comprehend the sound. He leans right into it, into the night, and shuts his eyes. Candles glow from little caves high up in the wall, and overlooking the room is a pop art depiction of a near-naked woman glancing over her shoulder. The waitress slides by with her hard braids and hips, and the musicians' eyes flicker when she passes, and passes again. The drummer pounds out something loaded and visceral, a rhythm of sacrificial rites and sex and breathing.

Some of the visiting musicians stop by the table and press Gabriel's hands like they are rubbing a buddha. He continues to rock and sway, following wherever the players want to go. He is let in on the grown universe, how adult desire is rendered. The sounds are relaxed, then turn tumultuous. The saxophonist snatches rage from the air and squeals it out: a grown man's supplication or a baby's terrible wail. Jazz is about the body, or having to take out the garbage; the sex that was had, or wasn't, the guy washing the streets with his grief, oranges tumbling from a grocery sack, or the edge of a chemical high; a flirt, or a flirt with suicide, or the way cigarette butts line up against the curb.

＊

The third way riffs on the pictorial language of Gabriel's *I-want* strips. My impulse is to collect images for a sentence I can't otherwise say. When I learn that there is an exhibit of polar landscape paintings at a museum in Massachusetts, a couple of hours away, I don't just want to see it, I *have* to see it. I have to see the Ice through the eyes and hands of others, see the place in my mind refracted through exterior lenses. Because this isn't just about the place, but also about the people who have found themselves alone in it.

When I tell R that I want all of us to go to Peabody for the exhibit, he's not surprised and he's always game for a family expedition, so soon enough the four of us are in the museum during February school vacation week. As I stand in a room with some of the polar landscapes, Gabriel is behind me, pretending not to see. He does this sometimes. He's never appeared to notice an airplane overhead or a kite. He won't turn and look when we point out a shark in a tank, an African mask, a mummy. Or perhaps he sees so much that he has to protect his autonomy, give every appearance of receding if it means slowing the pace of the newly revealed. So he fades his gaze as if he's standing in an empty room, and on the walls are pictures of snow, variations of empty. He lingers nearby, and parents and children flow in noisy streams around him. The parents look away, but the children sometimes stop in the din to stare at him, at the way that he is the same as them and yet—they seem to decide—not. I used to think the differences in his facial features and the way he walks and stands were subtle, but time has made them less so. The younger ones hang their mouths open for a few beats and then stagger away. He pretends he can't see them either. I press my face close to his and say, *You're so beautiful. You're so utterly beautiful.* He makes a clicking sound, which means he's satisfied—it is, I think, aside from his laughter, my favorite of his myriad sounds—and I turn back to the paintings.

Many of them were created when the edges of the polar regions were first being explored, and most have elements of the fantastic, are renderings based on captains' descriptions or approximations the painter could only have imagined and put together in the relative comfort of a studio. The repeated motif, painted in light that makes me think of Monet's Rouen cathedrals, is the crushed boat on vast floes and the survivors left to writhe out their existence under brooding, sometimes violent skies. But I'm not interested in their calamities, the fracturing black boats, and the suffocating closeness of men, and it's powerful to have the freedom to turn away.

I walk past images of the aurora, pulses of light held on heavy indigo paint, created long before anyone knew the sun could hurl solar winds at the Earth, make curtains of colored light hundreds of miles high. There are refracting suns along horizons, haloes and parheli, and ice in shades of turquoise, azure, and a bottle green that stop me, even crimson. Finally, I see it: *Icebergs, Davis Strait,* 1930, by one of Canada's Group of Seven painters, Lawren Harris. A depiction of the other end of the world from where Byrd was at more or less the same time; its near—but distinctly different—twin. The icebergs are striated in blues and whites, hold a muscular, totemic quiet. When Harris painted this, having been to the Arctic on a supply ship, he was married but in love with another woman; add to his dilemma the cusp of the Depression, coming war, the human furies then outside this view. The implied roar. I stay in front of it, this silence colliding with the noise of history and of schoolchildren, for a long time. The nights have been broken for so long at this point that I can't seem to locate the words for how tired I am, how inside myself. How I want to find my way out. I turn and look at Gabriel, his blue eyes with the bergs in them, and he looks straight back.

✳

Byrd calls flying in the Antarctic *flying in a bowl of milk*. I read this when I'm in bed, tucked beside my lamp with *Exploring with Byrd*, about his first expedition to the Ice, in 1928. He's been flying his plane in what he describes as a porcelain bowl, or this, which stops me: *Only a milky, trembling nothingness* (and I doubt that he consciously intends a sexual inference, but there it is). Eventually, he sees a mountain, and then a total of fourteen peaks, counts them out knowing that they will fill a blank on maps of Antarctica.

I read this and then fall asleep with the book in my hands. The membrane between space and time is a sieve; I can be dusted through it and reassembled on the other side. I don't know what it is that I'm seeing. There is a total lack of definition, and not the expected blinding Antarctic white but an impression of navy and umber and black. On my skin is a sparkling cold so searing it calls to mind fire and wakes me. In that flash of sleep, in a hot room, I had been freezing.

I get up and walk in the dark to Gabriel's room. Something about the silence seems noisy; it has a presence as distinct as calling. The dark has that pixilated look, as if it's full of flies or bees, and there's light at the bottom of his door. My image flicks by in the mirror at the end of the hall. Perhaps there are times when you know what you're about to find.

When I open his door, I find him slathered. He's sitting on his bed and his right hand is cradling feces the consistency of pudding, his hand cupped as though he's holding a small bird. His face is smudged, and on his quilt are several Rorschachs: a flying eagle, a vase, a topographical map. His pants and the back of his shirt are covered, too, and his eyes are wide as he watches me. My heart clinks faster as the air fills with the prickly scent of chaos. There is the clean glint of stars in the cold night, and this extravagant disaster, and the reconciling of the two together.

I can see him assessing my body language. Something in his expression suggests his fascination is not untouched by revulsion. It seems he's playing with contrasts, testing the way that his own interest comes up against an instinctive distaste, and waits for my response. He watches how still I am at the door, how I seem to be locked in a kind of momentary paralysis. I'm actually trying to think which piece of him to clean first.

I can almost hear the guy in *Cool Hand Luke* drawling, *What we have here is failure to communicate*. Somewhere in here is a zen koan about upheavals and their appearance, what a friend of mine calls *Another fucking growth opportunity*. This is the night's ideational equivalent of fallen republics, coups d'état.

I see him, as he really is. A boy vibrating with the inveterate desire to say. Wanting a conversation so badly that this is the transmission, the note in the bottle. Graffito. His hair is not as light as it once was, though underneath his bangs the white vestiges glow along the rim of his forehead. He has the softest chin in the world and skin so fair that the network of veins is visible in places. His teeth are a little motley, varying in size and shape and even color as if they came from different mouths, and they're hard to clean. He resists the twice-daily brushing, but R and I are persistent, and in a twist common to Down syndrome, he hasn't a single cavity. He is looking at me with those blue eyes, his head tilting as if he's listening for something, as if he's picking up distant signals. His limbs are slender, with astonishing joint laxity, but his belly is rounded; his legs are long like his father's. I asked R what he remembers most about the younger Gabriel, and he recalled the small round spectacles that are no longer needed, the way Gabriel would pat his leg to sign *dog*, how he would slide down the carpeted stairs on his stomach, the way he squealed when tobogganing or gleefully kicked down the block cities we had built with him. R would call him Godzilla.

I'm not sure that it's possible, in describing him physically, to move any closer to the more nebulous characteristics, the private, ungraspable ones. Perhaps the fecal covering obscures him. Can you see him or is he lost? I'm standing in my pajamas (bare-footed, rumpled), in the collisions of light and dark, and there's a space that occurs between me and the boy in the night but there's still connection. I think the word—something like nobility, humility, opportunity, presence—is soul. Or maybe the word is inspiration, or spirit. It's hard to see it. Somewhere in the late eighties and early nineties when I was attending university, painting was said to be dead, the novel too, and possibly the soul. Beauty was repudiated and the earnest despised unless later found to be ironic, and anything warm and fuzzy was left to scorch in the new ozone rip. We were young enough to think that people who had children had taken the easy route. I don't know if we had heard of autism, which is a strange thought, considering the prevalence of the word now. Anyway, soul as applied to this situation means that the unknowable and uncontainable have made their entrance. There is the dead of night, Louis Armstrong in mid-laugh on the wall, and the great brown birds, how they envelop the room, and then us. And yet care and love not only turn up, they expand. It means that when Gabriel is covered in shit, the disaster really isn't one, that what appears to be a slaughter of language and taboo is only the flipside of the haunting and beautiful void, the Great Emptiness, the bowl of milk. Peace.

This is the thing of night. We contain variations that come like jazz riffs and change again in daylight, when the presence of the rest of the world is felt. My caring for Gabriel in the night occurs on an island, a remote part of it without internet, cable, or radio receivers. I can't tell what he's thinking as he's gazing at me from his brown cloak, but it occurs to me how tenacious care is, how it will turn up even in this sequestered place with its buckets and soaps, its sleeves pushed up to the elbows to show hands that are toughened by the repetitions but also ready.

Except I'm not ready. Night has lost its perimeters, or it's me that blurs. I want to go back to sleep like a desert traveler wants water. I can't think straight or begin to sort the scope of the mess in front of me and the living creature inside it. The linear left the building long ago and we've been joined by the dendritic and decentralized. I've never been someone who passes out, but it seems that the perfect thing to do would be to fall comatose to the floor.

When Apsley Cherry-Garrard wrote his book about Robert Scott's famous last expedition, he wrote about a deep sleep that I would like to be engulfed by, the blank and obliterating kind, the kind where, on waking, there's a few seconds of forgetting that holds within it something like infinity and offers an expanding, nameless territory and an expanding, nameless self. The sleep Cherry-Garrard wrote about was induced by the Antarctic, one of its gifts to the explorers, where a summer blizzard would settle in and there would be nothing to do but curl inside the tent to wait it out in delicious slumber, one day, two days, three days, waking to eat and then descending back into the abyss. Later, he would write that what he would give for a good sleep was five years of his life.

The Ice

Out on the Barrier, Byrd goes topside to check on the aurora and finds it bland. It's around midnight and the moment when things suddenly vanish, or turn up. His phonograph is playing inside his hut, Beethoven's *Fifth Symphony*. He has left the door open so the music swells onto the Barrier. The aurora begins to unroll its drapes and shoot beams over the sky until, Byrd will record in his diary, what he sees and what he hears become the same. I imagine him standing in his furs and mukluks, leaned back a bit to take it all in, the aurora expanding and rippling, his trapdoor propped open, and the Barrier receiving Beethoven for the first time. In 1810, the great German Romantic and sometimes music critic, E. T. A. Hoffman, would hear the *Fifth* and write, *Radiant beams shoot through the deep night of this region and we become aware of gigantic shadows which, rocking back and forth, close in on us, and destroy all within us except the pain of endless longing.*

I play the *Fifth* for Gabriel one afternoon, while he sits on the bed, and turn up the volume so that he can enter the symphony the way he enters jazz. He listens, while keeping his body very still and his head cocked to the side; as the first movement proceeds to the second, he starts to rock. I imagine Beethoven composing, the pen's scratches and the ringing in his ears that dogs him as he goes deaf. In the last movement, he adds instruments that have been previously silent: trombone, piccolo, contrabassoon. Silent— but they get the finale. I picture him hunched over his work and irascible because of the growing deafness that he tolerates better while composing. He forges a trail for the musician or the listener to follow, even the ones two centuries later. He says, follow me or be lost in this place; he knows how to endure the deficits of the body, lovers who slip away, fury that bolts through him and necessitates his apologies, the need to have paper or a piece of slate so visitors can write down what they want to say because he can no longer hear them through the noise.

I watch Gabriel absorbing the sounds, how open and attentive his expression has become. What Beethoven seems to be saying to him, to Byrd, to me, to anyone who will listen, is *I hear something else and I will lead the way.*

✳

provisions

Gabriel has to be unpeeled, the bed stripped, the floor scrubbed, the windows opened. We're attended in the night by plastic bags, newspapers, soaps, latex gloves, and disinfectant. The pajamas, extracted inch by inch, are so far gone (under there somewhere is a pattern of snowboarders maybe, or hockey players; I haven't found such a thing as jazz pajamas), I decide to throw them out. Which feels extravagant. Which feels clean and resolute; also dark and slightly wicked—a skin of him I'm throwing away. I walk him gingerly to the bathroom over a newspaper path since his feet are covered also. The extent of the mess crowds us, along with the messes exactly like it in the future, though it seems that the remedy is conferred by easily available things. Soap and water. Since I'm hustling inside a scene that's vaguely apocalyptic, the thought occurs to me, what if they weren't available, what then? But the soap is lavender-scented, the water warm, and Gabriel is calm and quiet while I wash him. The past Gabriel is here, the baby who loved to be bathed, and then the toddler who hated it and churned in a slippery struggle. The future Gabriel is here, too, the one who is my size and then bigger, the one with stubble to shave. Together we work along the Möbius strip of care.

R and I have been obliged to be obsessed by how Gabriel's body works and doesn't, how it expresses again and again whatever maladaptation has occurred in his brain. His bowel movements in particular have become one of our principal concerns, often superseding intellectual development and communication in the queue for attention because if the bowels aren't working, then nothing is. Contrary to this episode of sprawling feces, constipation has been his near constant companion since toddlerhood. More than this, virtually every fundamental process required to live in relative comfort has, in his body, become complicated. Around the time that his words began their exodus, he turned from being a child who ate an unusually broad spectrum of food, especially vegetables, to narrowing what he would put in his mouth to yogurt, applesauce, pudding, and the occasional sandwich or French fry, a diet that unsurprisingly exacerbated the sluggishness of his bowels. Physiological examinations turned up nothing to explain the change; it was yet another way that our world created dissonance for him, it was another kind of turning away. He was often battling dehydration, too, because he refused to drink more than a few sips at a time, even once ending up in the hospital with a saline drip. After that, R and I had to haunt him with a syringe filled with juice that we would squirt into his mouth whenever he started refusing to drink, in an effort to ward off another hospital stay. We have pored over when he last defecated or drank until time has turned to units that rely on his systems. Five days since he's had a bowel movement, twelve hours since he's had a drink. But each thing stands in relation to everything else, and so this exorbitant display of feces in his room is actually preferable to the subjugation of our daily routines to constipation, and at some point, he simply started eating his old diet again, as if pastas and stews and curries and tagines were always what he preferred, as if he had never turned away.

After drying him off, I dress him in fresh pajamas and feel something like triumph. The term *closed circuit* comes to mind. Later on, I will look it up: *An electric circuit providing an uninterrupted, endless path for the flow of current.* So says *Oxford.*

Under *care*, it states, *1 worry, anxiety. 2 an occasion for this. 3 serious attention; heed, caution, pain.* Care, it seems, keeps accounts of its weight, what happens if there is a lapse in attention. On a separate occasion when I had been about to wash his hands, I had turned on the tap and his hands were in the stream. Except that my hands are always in the stream covering his, so that I can gauge the water temperature. This time, in one of those sliver-sized but haunting moments of parental negligence, I was preoccupied with something I don't recall and my hands weren't in the water. When I touched the stream, I realized it was too hot and pulled his hands away. His responses were working slowly, and so his face was blank and unfeeling at first. It seemed a fire ant was strolling languidly up his arm and over his shoulder before finally latching his brain. I remember bracing, waiting for what came: the grimace, and a soft, nearly silent cry. *Serious attention; heed, caution, pain.*

Gabriel isn't making any sounds as I take him back to bed. He shuffles his feet along the floor and has the loose saunter of the freshly bathed, as if the events leading to his washing never happened. I turn out lights as we go, or close them, as my Italian friends say. Gabriel's and my night language is a patchwork of signals and sensations, and the opening and closing of light. He tilts his head as he walks, opens and closes his mouth as if he's speaking softly. I'm too tired to speak, too finely drawn. The garbage bags and heaped blankets sit outside his room and he appears not to see them. He gets into bed, lying down as always on his stomach, and he seems heavy, as if he'll go to sleep quickly. If he does, it's likely that he'll curl his right arm under his head in exactly the way he did as an infant; exactly. Experiences accumulate within him, and not just the ones to which he is passive or held captive but the ones that fully belong to him, to his own awareness. He is aware of me. He regards me from his pillow with his one available eye; he is a casually breaching whale taking a last look before slipping under.

It is possible to feel that cleaning up shit is noble because he needs me to do it. It is possible to feel, at the same time as depletion, gratitude that is as big as the dark. I go to write *I am his mother*, except that what I write is *I am his other*.

Begin again.

I tend to think that if he spoke, the night, too, would be different. The spell broken. Night would seem cold and clean and beautiful again. I have stood on the lawn in November wearing five layers of clothes to watch the Leonid meteor showers, or bathe my face in moonlight, or simply to see how immense the sky is and experience that twinge of becoming tiny in its indifferent embrace as it twirls unstoppably. I've witnessed aurora borealis, too, when I was twenty-one and floating at night on an Ontario lake in a small rowboat. I slipped over the side to swim in black water, drifted on my back, the dark rim of pines seeming very close. Above me drifted the smudged galaxy, and Leo, Hercules, and Cassiopeia. I floated there, felt myself being erased in the lake's black ink. And there it was, a brilliant green rolling over the Earth's magnetic arc, one stream after another. And along with it, a physical presence, a silence, enveloping and dark and honed.

Counterpoint to the darkness is the image in my mind of the huge expanses of white that surround Byrd, but even these are unreliable, or maybe full of possibility. White, in the ice world, is white simply because it's expected to be—look again. Snow in darkness is quite often blue. The ice moves and shifts, and what appears white in daylight often isn't. That expert on the void, Apsley Cherry-Garrard, wrote about his expedition with Scott, *A White Day is so rare.* Light breaks inside the crystals, unleashing shades of blue and mauve and green, and Cherry added: rose-madder. Pink where snow algae blooms. Red where seals and penguins have been slaughtered.

✳

A man comes to replaster the stairwell walls, and he shakes slightly. I didn't think he was coming, would ever show up in fact, but weeks after the initial quote he appears, smiling and ready to work as if this has been the plan all along. He is thin and wrinkled and makes me think of Keith Richards. I imagine that in his other life, when he isn't plastering, he wears sunglasses.

The walls' solidity isn't in doubt, but the surface is a wreck. At one time, there was an angry floral wallpaper that stretched from the bottom of the main floor to the top of the second, and finally I had gotten around to removing it after taking down the other ornate wallpaper in the house. Because it was daunting, I'd saved this area for last, and had perched on scaffolding to work at it, only to find that underneath the paper were thick areas of old paint that possibly date back to when the house was built in 1973. The patches, colored an inoffensive café au lait, lift around the edges but won't otherwise budge. When the plasterer speaks, gesturing at the islands of paint and tilting his head back to look up toward the ceiling, there are long pauses where he appears to visit some distant planet before resuming. He seems frail and smells of cigarettes. His brother, who worked on our bathrooms and discovered under the vanity that the builders had written in red marker *this house built by a bunch of pot smoking clowns*, is fat and robust and prone to commenting on my skirt or my hair.

The plasterer props the front door open, goes to his truck and hauls out buckets and drop cloths, arranges his tools while clomping about in his work boots. Once everything is in place, there is a pause, the master inhaling before he gets to work. Then he begins mixing and sweeping fresh plaster over the walls and I don't want to disturb him. I leave the house and when I return hours later, he is gone and there is just the crisp white of drying plaster. Two days later he comes to sand the walls, which he does entirely without a mask. He heats his foam coffee cup in the microwave. He drifts off in his speech again, appears to go missing, flickers back into view, and is gone again.

I keep coming out to the stairwell to feel the white walls' entirely new presence. There isn't a seam anywhere, crevice or trowel mark. Just this astonishing white surface.

People keep asking what color I'm going to paint the walls. I abandon all the color cards I've collected and go back to the paint store. It seems obvious to me what I should do, as the blank, this intriguing silent elegant blank, seems to call for more of the same. But you know by now that white isn't really white, and ice isn't just ice, and that a blank, like flypaper, gathers things to it, and so you look, and look again, and there is always more. I gather up the variations of color slips, stuffing them into my pockets: Frost, Snow, Rice Paper, Studio White, Popcorn, Whitecap, Journal, and Goalpost. Also: Brilliance, Lightning, Fresh Start, and Nirvana. Possibility. Whipping Cream and Whitewash. Whiteout.

provisions

The books about Antarctica turn up on the steps or are wedged in the storm door by men from UPS trucks, typically after 4 p.m. I recognize the purr of the trucks as they pull in and then away. Ordering the books has become a bit of a ritual, a way of receiving this distant but vivid place, a way to govern its presence by summoning them one or two at a time, the books that tend to have a penguin or a berg or a ghost-ship on the cover.

The problem with this sort of exploration, aside from the way that it can communicate only certain aspects of the experience of being there, is that the books tend to hew to the periphery, which is generally where the animals and plants are, because how, really, do you write a book about a blank? The periphery is cold enough but almost baroque with detail: lichens and mosses and stout flowers, cacophonous birds and seals, and icebergs that tour the seas like cruise ships, except bigger (much bigger). There is an algae that turns the snow pink and a fish with white blood. The coastal water's comparative warmth seeps into the cracks in the ice, causing its disintegration, frills the berg bottoms with enough sustenance for creatures to dwell, while the entire collection of pack ice turns in ancient rotations propelled by ocean currents. Add to this the absurdities of contrast: huge ice shelves composed of tiny crystal prisms and the whales that sustain themselves on krill.

It is the blank to the south, though, its sameness and lunar severity, that haunts us, though students of ice will list the variants they find, the rub of proximity that cleaves tabular bergs from shelves, growlers from bergy bits. They will rattle off: frazil ice, congelation ice, infiltration ice, undersea ice, ice cakes, pancake ice, ice bastions, shore ice, ice that is vuggy or rotten or fringed; blue ice, green ice, dirty ice, and brash ice; ice in rinds and folds and pinnacles. Ice that looks like pencils, or bullets. Ice that basically keeps its minute distinctions endless under a curtain of simplicity.

The South Pole, reached by calculation, is a figment of a beating heart. The universe comprehends itself through its living beings, extending only a few humans onto the ice, nudging the filthy, clumsy, and slow-moving creatures deeper into the landscape to reach the center. Endpoints here are achieved by celestial calculations and tallies and reckoning. The humans say, *hereabouts*, and stick their pins. Roald Amundsen, in December 1911, was the first to do this, arriving a month ahead of Robert Scott. He left nothing to chance, making a radius of twelve miles around his guess of the Pole's exact location, so he could say with some certainty: *we are here*. When he and his men were getting close to the Pole and about to be the first humans to claim it, they made a stop where the dogs sniffed toward the scentless South as though, Amundsen wrote, there was *something remarkable to be found there*.

Robert Scott did not follow Amundsen's example and use dogs on his journey—some of which, with painful hearts, Amundsen's men had finally eaten—but had starving, depleted men instead, and they came upon the Pole about a month later, only to find Amundsen's dark flag already there. It is an ironic idea that the Pole can be claimed, because what else is there to do but reckon a spot and run toward it? The first to see is the first to own, except that in this place, everything moves in its invisible rotations, the cycle of crystals from the interior out through the ice pack, as the ice heads blindly but unceasingly to the distant sea, hauling any pins in the map with it.

Prior to Byrd's second expedition, in 1933, the pack ice was the scene of entrapments and slaughters. The ravaging of fur seals in the early nineteenth century was a long red gash over the Ice that nearly extinguished the species and left other wounds behind it. Sailing southwest of the Antarctic Peninsula, the crew of the *Belgica* in 1898 became ensnared in the pack and, wintered over, suffered the night with scurvy and madness. On the expeditions of Shackleton and Scott, ponies and sledge dogs perished or were killed by their owners for food; Amundsen was mesmerized by the cutlets of what were once his dogs being trimmed and laid out on the snow. Curious seals and penguins that wandered too close to the men's camps met a similar fate. And faced with the Ice's simplicity, the Nazis flew their planes over it and shed a black rain of swastika flags. The flags, no doubt, suffered the same fate as everything else, buried in drift and moved inch by inch to the sea.

So there is Byrd in his suffering, on the Barrier, and all around him a moat of crystals.

The periphery's elaborations, the exposed rocks and wild seas and trapped ships, are long gone, and even the crammed world he tried to bring with him and store in his hut is dwindling. The place he inhabits now is a honed one that doesn't refer to humans but to the general absence of them. An absence, in turn, that could be investigated only by a single person.

✳

When I lie in the dark, I try to remember the light, hold on to it, to my daily runs when the sun is coming up or going down; the day when I ran through the woods along the ocean and the falling sun lit the trees sideways with orange spots that looked like trail blazes, so that it wasn't until my shadow erased them that I understood they hadn't been painted on. And the autumn day that had been as dim as a burrow, the ocean had looked like lead, and most of the leaves were down, but I found some maples still dangling their light high up; they were black sentries with yellow campaign flags. And the times R and I have sat on the beach with the boys in late afternoon just to experience the light turn peach and gold and the illuminated grasses hold back the dunes. I stroke these moments like rosary beads.

provisions

There was the morning R and I went to New York City without the boys—we went by train, riding along light-saturated, weedy Connecticut fields, past graffiti and junkshops and wetlands, which always seem to me like the *behind* of things, like being backstage except well lit. We'd wandered through Central Park, past marathoners and a man wearing a bath towel praying fervently on the sidewalk, facing the rising sun. There was something remarkable about the sun that day—that when setting, it would align itself with the cross streets, fully illuminating them in long slices; the effect, occurring twice yearly, has been dubbed *Manhattanhenge*.

We got into the Metropolitan Museum of Art before the crowds only just beginning to gather at the main entrance, and wandered through the galleries, which seemed larger and stranger than usual because, except for the guards, we were alone. I wanted to see the iris painting by Van Gogh—one of the two that he mentions in his letter to his brother, Theo, in May 1890. *At the moment the improvement is continuing, the whole horrible crisis has disappeared like a thunderstorm, and I'm working here with calm, unremitting ardor to give a last stroke of the brush. I'm working on a canvas of roses with a bright green background and two canvases of large bouquets of violet irises, one lot against a pink background in which the effect is harmonious and soft through the combination of greens, pinks, violets. On the contrary, the other violet bouquet (ranging up to pure carmine and Prussian blue) standing out against the striking lemon yellow background with other yellow tones in the vase and the base on which it rests is an effect of terribly disparate complementaries that reinforce each other by their opposition.*

I imagined that Van Gogh wasn't sleeping much at the asylum in St. Remy in 1890. He would soon be dead. I stood in front of the irises and watched them as though waiting for a camouflaged bird to move and reveal itself. Of the two works mentioned in his letter, the one in the museum was the one with the pink background. Or rather, at one time it was pink, but was now just about completely white. So not-pink, in fact, that the viewer wouldn't know simply by standing in front of it that the background used to be a different color, so nearly complete was the transformation. The explanation for such an absence, as written on the information card attached to the wall, was *owing to a fugitive red pigment.*

The words were almost as magnetic to me as the painting. A red in the act of fleeing. In the act of being unreliable, maybe hiding. There, and gone. Red, despite its volatility, despite being errata, and arousal, a pumping heart, was—in the painting anyway—retreating. Van Gogh had merged a dollop with obliterating white to create the pink he intended—pink, which is erasure and rapture. His gesture had been full of intention; he'd meant to enforce a kind of harmony. Was the change something he anticipated, as he was well versed in colors' transposing nature? Maybe he understood well enough that the motion he extended into the painting would be instable, something living. The paint that was now white held a secret, one about mutability.

I could stand before the painting as the sleepless parent of a wordless child and make these sorts of connections, teasing out the weakest threads between seemingly isolated and irrelevant occurrences and tying them together until they meant something. I can't say why I would do this, only that it occurs in the same way that weather happens or tides, though to make the connections, I suppose, is to bear witness, to become a conduit for a language without words. There is a supposition at work that meaning wants to be found. When I was standing in front of Van Gogh's irises, just about eclipsing the entire show was the behavior of red and something about the nebulous territories we believe to be ours. Something, too, about another force concentrating its will upon one. In the emptied background, then, a simple truth of our situation, that unreliability is an essential trait of what is living.

＊

R and I, along with friends, take Gabriel to a different jazz club, this one in New London, Connecticut, about an hour from our house. We've been here a few times before. I walk Gabriel through the puzzle of bodies on the club's upper level, which is a sports bar, to get downstairs to our table in the basement, where the floor is a gray mesh of footprints and every surface is sticky. Fries come in plastic baskets with wax paper liners, and the light fixtures don't match. A brick wall on one side is topped by chain link and colored lights and seems faintly like a psych ward at Christmas. The room, painted deep red, is long and narrow, and the band—sax, trumpet, drums, stand-up bass, and piano—fits on a small stage about six inches off the ground, and looks out to an audience that wakes around 10 p.m. The musicians wear jackets and ties and, in his other life, the guy leading them with his trumpet is an emergency room doctor. The sound for him must be full of subtlety or sirens.

They play "Sandu" by Clifford Brown, and the deeper they go, the more alleys appear. A passing train hoots its hollow blast into the club, and the sound links with the horns before fading. Baby Grand Davis pinches some dissonance from the piano with his right fingers, then does a melodic slide down the keys that moves him straight off his seat and almost onto the table of two women who are seated near the stage. He mugs at them, pulls himself back in, and the band is jumping. It's like the stage is a griddle with water drops bouncing on it. Gabriel isn't rocking and clapping as he usually is, he is utterly transfixed.

Hoagy Carmichael talked about a night in 1923, at a black-and-tan joint, listening to and then joining in on piano with cornetist Bix

Beiderbecke. *He showed me that jazz could be musical and beautiful as well as hot. He showed me that tempo doesn't mean fast. His music affected me in a different way. Can't tell you how—*
like licorice, you have to eat some.

A radio announcer called Monk's music extraordinary, in spite of him *playing the wrong notes on the piano.* Monk dropped notes from his chords like he was shucking peas, and within the newly created space the remaining notes joined edgily to create his signature sound. There was this and his silences, hesitations like colors. Monk called the station switchboard: . . . *the piano,* he said, *ain't got no wrong notes.*

Hoagy Carmichael: *It was the music. The music took me and had me and it made me right.*

✳

S's friend A is over at the house. A is the kind of kid who's going to educate him on a few things, throw light into some dark corners. The first time A's mother dropped him off, she was heading back down the walkway when she turned and said, *Oh . . . Don't let him near any matches.* For Hallowe'en, before she'd put a stop to the idea, he wanted to be a pimp. When I took them out to lunch one day, he perused the cocktail menu while laughing heartily.

S and A are playing upstairs while I'm in the kitchen, moving between occupying Gabriel and chopping vegetables. I hear S run down the stairs, a pause and a rustle close by me, then the *thup-thup-thup* as he runs back up. A few feet away from me, just around the corner, a crackling sound materializes, the intimations of distance and far-off places. I find the walkie-talkie he's put on the floor and pick it up. His transmission then: *We're thirsty*. I think of Byrd, and also Monk, his incident in the Delaware Hotel with the water and the silence.

He'd stopped at the hotel and walked into the lobby because he wanted a drink of water. According to the hotel owners, who called the police, he just stood there, saying nothing. There was silence as heavy as armor and the owners delivering their rage to the black man in need of something. 1958. You have to admit, silence shakes things up.

Only months before, Monk had played Carnegie Hall with Dizzy Gillespie, Billie Holiday, Ray Charles, and Sonny Rollins, among others; he'd played the Newport Jazz Festival, been photographed by *Esquire* and the subject of a profile in *Downbeat* magazine after winning the critics' poll. Then there he was, thirsty and saying nothing.

His friend Nica—Pannonica, the baroness who'd been driving him to Baltimore in her Bentley—told the police officers that he was ill. (In another six months, he would come late to a gig, sleepless and wild with pacing, would play and pace, then sit at the piano without moving until all of his musicians, Rouse and Jones and Taylor, had gotten off the stage and left. It was possible for him to sit and cause an unfolding all around him.)

She told them he was ill, and the police officers replied that they should leave, but then they followed the Bentley along the highway and pulled them over. Monk tucked into his silence as he held the car door and one of the cops started beating him, beating his hands. A drumming of hands and sticks, and a gap in the night.

There is another story, too, of Manhattan covered in snow and Monk sliding his Buick into the back of another car. He slid into the car, and then his silence, which provoked the other driver. Snow, and silence. The police came to get him and took him to a hospital. On his car, his beloved Buick Special, they left a piece of paper:

Psycho taken to Bellevue.

＊

At the market where I shop, there's a woman, J, with a vague disability who bags the groceries. She's probably forty-five or fifty years old and, in the current parlance, she is high functioning. She smiles enormously when she recognizes her customers, then looks through her thick glasses as if down a well and begins slowly to bag the items. On a recent day, the clerk who was operating the cash register and who was apparently annoyed, snapped to J that there were already cloth bags in front of her, she didn't need to use the plastic. J drew out a slow smile and said amiably, *Oh . . . okay,* and gingerly opened a cloth bag. The clerked hissed and jerked a box of pasta across the scanner. I watched how J, unruffled, continued her careful process, placing a few items in the cloth bags before returning to the plastic ones. I saw something I recognized, the retreat with the hint of defiance, a wall around her. The back-and-forth between the clerk and J unfolded as if pasta and apple juice were symbols of will and acquiescence. J finished filling the bags, lifted them into the shopping cart. I saw a flicker of humor, and we grinned at each other.

Autonomy finds a way. Gabriel's autonomy expanded with his discovery of willful sitting. Or the plop-and-sit, if we're out walking somewhere. He's been known to settle to the ground in the middle of parking lots, sidewalks, beaches, and dirt trails. Or if he's already sitting, he can refuse to stand. It seems when he does it that there's an essential honesty, not because he isn't capable of subterfuge, or can't understand mischief or sleight of hand, but because his alternative language, in the instance of rebel sitting, uses his whole body; he embodies defiance with a whole note. I know its power because both R and I have stood in impotent rage before it, panicked to find ourselves unable to move him, have him do what seems so important at that moment for him to do. Like Monk, he can cause an unraveling all around him.

Gabriel and I listen one night to Monk's "Blue Bolivar Blues" in R's and my bedroom, and I sit down on the bed with him, being careful to stay close to the edge. As much as silence is a function of his being, so is space, and he sometimes needs a good deal of it. The bed, when he's listening, is his. It is possible for me, faced daily with his interior rules, to want to flout them—sometimes you just want to sit on the bed. My presence beside him intrigues him, then it seems to disturb him. It's a familiar scenario, with the usual loops and repetitions, set to Monk's upbeat tune (which Monk also named "Bolivar Blues" and "Ba-Lue Bolivar Ba-Lues-Are"; one of the places his friend Nica lived was the Bolivar Hotel). His focus shifts from Monk to me, as he reaches across the white duvet to my leg and touches it, gently at first, stroking my pant leg, before starting to try to move me. The white space is an ice floe that has gone unnoticed until he indicates it, shows me it's there. I stay a moment, despite knowing he'll be held in the grip of one of his thought circles until I get up. Typically, I try to keep him out of the loops or break them as soon as possible by distracting him—anything simple will work: singing a song, giving him a drink, moving him to another room, or in this case, if I simply get off the bed, he'll stop. But I stay there a bit longer, watching his eyes, which have become black, and his electrified focus while Monk plays in our ears, in part because I'm having a moment of my own—I'm tired and just want to sit on the damn bed—and because I want to examine the space and his reaction, find what they mean. That there is possibly no meaning to be found doesn't seem to bother me. Somewhere in the tiniest particles of the space is the secret. *Okay, Gabe, okay*, I say. *I'm up.*

Did Monk control the silence, or did it control him? Perhaps it was both. His father spent the last years of his life in a mental institution, suffering from some of the same things that afflicted Monk. But Monk had his music, a way of conversing with the silence. Sometimes he would get up during a gig and dance around, which meant he thought the band was swinging. And he had Nellie, his wife and support. He would sweat when he played, and so Nellie made him large white handkerchiefs with which he could wipe his face, and sometimes when he got up to dance, he'd unfurl one of these flags. His surrender.

The Ice

It is the last day of May, and Byrd has a radio schedule with his men, which means running the generator in his tunnel. Listening to the distant voices on his radio receiver, he conducts business with Little America for an hour and a half, sending back his hesitant code until it occurs to him that the engine doesn't sound right. *Wait,* he spells, and goes to check. He is snuffed like a flame. When he regains consciousness, he reaches for the telegraph key and through a heavy veil, signs off, though he can't get the earphones back on his head to know whether Little America has responded. Dizziness and nausea rumble through and his heart surges.

In the scramble of memory and time, he finds himself lying on his bunk. He wakes enough to understand that the engine is still running. Crawling under the exhaust clouds, he is finally able to reach it and shut it down; crawls again to his stiff sleeping bag and shifts himself in.

Later he will write, . . . *the illusion of being a thin flame drawn between two voids.*

✳

When I'm here in the dark, I wish on the stars for what seems like their detachment, their delicious remove. What looks like a kind of freedom. But the twinkling is a bit of a ruse, attached as it is to a thread that stretches back into a sink of millions of years. Somewhere back in time their cores rage. Night's ancient blasts and fires that are now so refined the cacophony is lost, combustion turning cold and clean and inscrutable. I want, sometimes, a night like this.

figment [no.1]

Running around the edge of the pond, I see the hunched form of the fox, exposed in daylight as though sleeping in grass. A few flies thread the air around her as I look more closely to assess how still she is, how dead. I watch and wait, wondering the protocol. Do you speak to the dead? Say a prayer? I whisper, and improbably the fox lifts her head, carefully turning her small painted face toward me, her eyes shut tight as fists. She is not yet dead. I feel like Alice, like I've grown larger and larger until I'm forced to back away and slip around the other side of the pond, taking my presence and intrusions with me. I walk in an arc, sitting down on the grass many yards away, obscured by foliage. But after I watch her dying for a while, she lifts her head in my direction, smelling where I am, so I pull away again. She is not to be watched, and I run back to the path, slip back into the forest.

3 a.m.

*

white

＊

Dear Mom and Pops,

This is going to be bad news and here it is, our class is going to slay our plants. Do you know what slay means? These plants were meant to die. First we grow them and act like we love them, then after a while we . . . have them Die. So, that is what this paragraph is all about.

love, S

＊

S is afraid of the dark. There is a sharp glow around his door that illuminates the end of the hall. He sleeps under the glare of his ceiling light and not one but two bedside lamps, which R and I sneak in to turn off before we go to bed. At some point during the night, he gets up and turns them back on. But all this is fairly new; when he was a baby and toddler, he slept fearlessly in the dark. There are no streetlamps or neon signs here to leak in. Only a low full moon, especially if there's snow cover, will spill inside so that it's possible to move around without a light. Otherwise, the black is a palpable element. Once he reached a certain age, it seemed that he understood that he entered his dreams alone. How vulnerable the sleeping body is, how left behind. Paralyzed and private. He could no longer float trustingly into sleep with everything dark around him and so in order to go to bed, he arms himself with light, layers of it in every lamp around him. He has nearly unbroken sleeps, and R and I don't hear from him until morning. When I told my therapist about his impervious slumbers she said, *He knows who has the night.*

Of course, I'm afraid of the dark, too. The problem is the range of possibility, the way exploration has to be done by feel before finding the lamp. My recurring dream as a child: feeling through a dark room for the light switch and finding that it doesn't work. The dark is the sovereign country of the unknown, and a borderless one, at that. The guards are just glimpses and shapes. Striking a light is only so helpful when the light is artificial, an intruder. The dark hunkers down in the self-satisfied comprehension that it is the one, and the only one, at home.

But what I'm afraid of now, aside from the dark, is interruptions in the dark. I wake even when Gabriel sleeps, just because I'm anticipating getting up. The anxiety becomes too large, almost as if the interruption arrives not from him but through him, as if the universe is transmitting its own impatience, the primacy of its need. When he breaks the night or hovers expectantly in daylight, it's electric and impossible to ignore. He's a tsunami of interruption, a forty-foot wall of it. We can only allow him to pass over, loaded with boats and houses and drifting people, awash in the force of him and the resulting debris to which we'll have to attend.

And then I think I must have it wrong. Byrd, even in his misery, looks out to the night around him, in which he is entirely alone, and he watches the sky. The aurora unfolds, both sinister and beautiful, and he feels a harmony with the things that normally lie beyond his attention; he is lifted out of himself and spends a moment or two where he understands all that he needs to before he begins again to forget. The dark is the fulcrum for that harmony—the aurora is invisible without it. So, too, the stars.

It took years to see that Gabriel was unlike anyone we knew, until we finally understood that no one was either so magical or so lost to behavioral repetitions. Bound by increasing cycles and loops, he would repeat an action without seeming to tire of it. Aside from shrieking episodes and night waking, he would throw or bang an object, or rock back and forth, or jump up and down for long periods, and like the disappearance of his words, the accumulation was gradual and almost lulling.

There was a space when he was very little where we caught our breath. The seizures were gone and the crying, too, and he emerged from that spell a round, beaming baby, one year old. There were the first ripples of conversation, the first sightings that we took to be him, the authentic him (which was erroneous, of course, because he has always been the authentic him). I remember that in the autumn of that year, R and I took him camping to Algonquin Park, a huge Ontario forest, and how extraordinary and ordinary this seemed. We showed him moose standing in streams, enormous beaver dams, the lit halls of hemlock cathedrals, and lakes old enough to be dying. We hiked under beech trees where black bears had nestled in the branches and feasted on the seeds. At night, guides organized wolf calls so that the humans could converse with the wolves, but it was just a distant, floating language. The wolves were peripheral and cloaked, and we never caught a glimpse of them. Two weeks after returning home, we read in the *Globe and Mail* about a couple and their toddler camping just a few miles from where we'd been; a wolf had lunged into their camp, grabbed the child by the abdomen, and tossed him in the air before fleeing. The boy had escaped injury. I wondered about him, about the story he would have to tell when he grew up, how a wolf had grabbed him, and he flew.

As Gabriel grew, he seemed to become more entranced by his repetitions, the most notable, because the most onerous, being his shrieking, but he began to practice an entire language of obsessions and sameness, one that expresses his uneasiness with his body and all the world's *things*. Throwing began, and the swinging of doors open and shut, and sometimes hitting himself in the head. It's like watching someone with an impaired memory wake every day to a new world, one that he has to examine and repudiate all over again. Various sensory therapies followed, attempts to ease the exchanges between him and everything else. When he was still small, we massaged his limbs and swept a soft brush over his body, a process called the Wilbarger Protocol, which is meant to alleviate sensory discomfort, and used vibrating toys on his hands for the same reason. We took him for cranio-sacral therapy, where a man gently massaged Gabriel's skull, and hired a private occupational therapist to create an at-home program to help him acclimate to the routine tasks of daily living and their attendant objects: the use of a spoon, a cup, a toothbrush, a hairbrush. He seemed to enjoy the therapies, and providing them made R and I feel less helpless, but his repetitions and what seems like sensitivities in his hands have continued. The mysteries of language and communication have become knotted up with the presence of the body and objects within a space. Watching him repeatedly dismantle the contents of a drawer, for instance, makes me think that he isn't only playing in the way a toddler does when emptying the kitchen cupboards but that something more philosophical is happening and he is working out the puzzle of the material world, the *thingness* of things. In some ways, it's gratifying to see him sit on the floor beside a chest of drawers and pull T-shirts and pants into heaps around him because it does seem like playing, connected as it is to the development of typical babies. But he is far from being a baby now, and the relentless focus on his task reminds R and me that we are all a bit stuck. The clothes heap, like Sisyphus' rock, suggests we are chained to a process of repacking drawers, to righting and repairing things.

*

Gabriel throws. He throws magazines, stuffed bears, plastic plates, pillows, storybooks, pens, toast, peanut butter sandwiches, puzzle pieces, playing cards, and lamps.

Also CDs, DVDs, DVD players, blankets, toothpaste tubes, hairbrushes, toy cars, Lego pieces, crayons, and picture symbols.

Shoes, socks, pants, turtlenecks, nail clippers, novels, and cheese cubes.

Pretzels, building blocks, French fries with ketchup, cups with juice, bagels with cream cheese.

Staplers, tree-shaped candleholders, comic books, atlases, high-heeled dancing shoes, prescription sunglasses.

Paper napkins, bowls of yogurt, bowls of popcorn, bowls of pudding, and bowls.

Buttons, butter knives, orange slices, apple pieces, paper clips, camera parts, and magnets.

And balls. He throws balls.

If you want to be with him, converse with him, live with him, you must be willing to be with the repetitions also. They're something he's trying to say. Which doesn't mean that I'm always available to hear it. The repetitions are deafening, deadening, and simple. Sisyphus' trek with his rock is not complicated; it's precisely the simplicity and the anticipation of the next cycle that generates the mien dark enough to be mythological. When the repetitions come in their spare but unceasing waves, I experience something very much like self-pity. I read a few words in a book, and he taps his sentence strip on my shoulder or leans over me as I sit in a chair and a long drip of saliva falls from his mouth (which, because I'm his mother, and in spite of the frustration, I sometimes find elo-quent). Or he stamps his foot or makes a sound, a whine or a moan, or he taps his yes/no sign. I fulfill his requests, read a few words more, try to center myself in the spot I was, and hear the television remote shatter on the living room floor or cutlery clatter and spin on the kitchen tile, or S's books and drawings being swept from the table. The rest of us insist, regardless of knowing better, regardless of knowing his thoroughly entrenched repetitions, on continuing to place our books and drawings on the table, the TV remote out in the open in the living room. (And the TV remote has a story of its own; aside from being held together with tape, it has also lived for its own protection inside a plastic container; until Gabriel learned to open plastic containers, and we found him, giddy with triumph, sitting on the sofa with the remote.) We insist on flouting his rules because our habits are more like his than we care to admit, because repetition is comforting in some way, or it's a way of insisting on having our way, and so we suffer a loop of our own.

I was chopping vegetables while he sat and ate his cheese cubes, a magazine on the tabletop beside him. Magazines are one of his tantalizers. Eventually the cheese was gone, but the magazine remained. I saw, as so many times before, how he reached for it, slowly and subtly, his fingertips finally touching down and the almost luxurious tugging on the paper. The magazine turned fluid as it spilled over the table edge and resolidified before it hit the tile.

I have wanted to open the repetitions, see the insides. His experiments are ones of extension: how to place the urges in his body into the atmosphere and see the consequence in the people around him. The variations are exquisitely minute, and endless. Thousands of incidents—pullings, tuggings, throwings—and an equal number of responses. R and I are practiced at the poker face, the slow breathing, the nonchalance, but if the repetitions show us anything it is how human we are, how fallible. There is always a time when we react more than we intended, or when his faulty vision is suddenly so attuned that he detects the ripple of frustration, a sweat droplet on the brow. Examining the repetition does nothing; there is only more of the same.

✳

When Gabriel was still a small baby, small enough that R and I believed that by receiving various nutritional and educational therapies, he would surpass the low expectations other people had of his development, long before he exhibited behaviors that moved him from one diagnosis into another, I went with a friend to visit an older couple and their grown son with Down syndrome. At the time, I thought I was coming to see the future, what Gabriel would in some way be like. D was in his early thirties and, dressed in a button-down shirt and khakis, went into the kitchen to make us coffee. He rode the transit system by himself and had a job. He griped about the people he worked with. He showed me his computer where he was entering word-for-word the pages of a book he liked. He stuttered severely, and at the time—unaware of just how accomplished he was—I thought it was somewhat tragic how much time and patience were required to hear him. The stuttering seemed like a barrier to the man who was so well developed and thoughtful, and I was inexperienced enough not to see that, in the grand scope of impairments, it was incidental.

His chief love was for musicals, and he went to see as many as possible, his favorite being *The Wizard of Oz*. He had an old hardcover edition of the book that he showed me while telling me about seeing the musical version at a nearby theater. I asked him who was his favorite character, and he answered, *Oh, the Wizard,* and described the scene where the Wizard is discovered to be just a man. He struggled over his words, but they were there—the very elusive creatures I would love to hear now from Gabriel—one halting sound at a time. *I feel like that sometimes,* he said.

I'm a very good man . . . I'm just not a very good wizard.

I'm not a very good wizard either.

I have watched Gabriel's favorite spot in the living room became more and more featureless as we've negotiated the territory with him and made our modifications. In some ways our freedoms have shrunk in accordance with his (though freedom is a relative concept; we likely can't grasp either the degree to which his freedoms are lost, or the surprising ways that he might be freer than we are). Certain drawers are kept locked or emptied because of his raiding, and loose objects kept out of reach. Where the coffee table once stood, there's now nothing. The walls are bare and the end tables, too. (It's okay, I've discovered, for us to be bitter about the adaptations, and it's also okay to note that the need for them has made us increasingly resourceful. Also less cluttered.) We don't tend to collect things—the miniature or the fragile or the found—to bring home; no groups of shells or vases or figurines, though we do have shelves stuffed with books. In the arbitrary rules of his obsessions, there are certain things that are exempt from his notice, and the books fall into this category; so, too, Christmas trees.

In the absence of a ceiling light, there was, however, a lamp. Because of the room's configuration, the lamp had to sit on a small table not far from the sofa, close to the spot where he curls up or stands and bounces. It was seductively large, made of gleaming metal with a pleated white shade, and he discovered that he could crash it, breaking the bulb, or tip it slowly, so that it fell almost elegantly, gaining momentum before hitting the floor. Sometimes the light would stay on and draw taut his interest. He repeated the process with every righting of the lamp, which stayed more or less intact, though sometimes he ignored its presence for days at a time only to remember it and begin again.

Begin again. We didn't understand. He was five years old when he started to shove the lamp, and he continued for two years. It was like finding a new hieroglyph and peering at it with a headlamp and held breath to try to figure out what the hell it meant. Because that was it: its meaning and how to get him to stop. We wondered what was the word for this, because it became apparent that there had to be one, that he had stepped with his repetitions from one circle into another. It seemed to us that he was so unlike anyone else we knew, even other children with developmental delays, that a moat had formed around us; we were, all of us, isolated.

The lamp found itself in an unbreakable loop of being repaired or righted and set back on the table for the next attack. That side of the room was too dark without it, and so there seemed to be nothing to do but answer Gabriel's repetitions with our own. Perhaps, also, the sparse surroundings had gotten to us, and we wanted to insist on this one last thing: light. We wanted him to learn to live with it. For two years, psychology and science were applied to the question posed by his behavior. Functional analyses were performed and combed over and modifications practiced, as if this was the way to break his code, break him, and find meaning in the meaningless. I thought, witnessing his passionate persistence, that there had to be a reason.

I wondered afterward who was persisting more, the child or the adults?

Then one day I was standing in the doorway watching him, the puzzle I couldn't solve. There was the warm, dim light of early evening, and I stood there watching him watching the lamp. He touched the tight pleats of the shade gently, stroking them as though they belonged to something living. He pulled his hand away, shifting from foot to foot, and reached out to the folds once more, the alternating light and shadow, and it happened again: the hardening of his expression, his hand making contact, the crashing lamp and darkness.

Darkness, except that I understood what I hadn't before, that he was struggling. He had been trying, all that time, to stop himself from toppling the lamp. But it was a moon yanking a tide. There, in his skirmish with the lamp's magnetic pull, he was entirely alone. Desire, unabashedly, won. I wanted him to stop being alone.

So I relinquished all the postulations and remediations and attempts to get him to stop, and did something simple: I bought a new lamp. It was virtually identical, except that it was the kind that bolts to the wall. So R got out his drill and carefully measured and, while Gabriel watched with interest, shifting from foot to foot, he installed it. And as simply as that, the lamp and Gabriel have lived peacefully since.

✳

R: *How was school?*
S: *Yes. And no.*
R: *Did you have fun?*
S: *Nothing.*

This is the theater of the absurd that unfolds in our kitchen. S, who has discovered the world of codes, grins wildly and scrambles for a piece of paper and crowds over it with his pencil like Glenn Gould at a piano. He gives the paper to R, who can see that N-O-T-H-I-N-G has been written backwards, and so to be properly perceived, the paper has to be held up to a mirror. Which S, cackling maniacally, exhorts him to do. He runs for another paper, works furiously, and delivers the next message, this time with *Nothing* written in code, complete with an alphabet key underneath. He squirms with pleasure while R and I decipher the Nothing. More loud chortling as he goes off to create another code.

Even though S can make anything ambiguous, yes-and-no has a delicious clarity. We had tried for a long time to find a way for Gabriel to express it reliably. But his neck muscles have low tone, and his headshakes and nods are often hard to discern from each other. Two kinds of electronic communication devices had been tried, neither very successful nor good enough to replace his picture symbols. His teachers decided to innovate, and since separate yes-and-no cards hadn't worked, they made him a single card with two squares, one containing yes and the other no, and taught him to use it by asking him question upon question about topics he loves and rewarding him immediately for a response. R and I have considered this simple innovation as one of the most profound acts of his schooling. We can't ask him, Did you dream last night about a dragon? or did the car horn frighten you? or is there a rock in your shoe? and get, necessarily, a response. As with constructing sentences using his picture symbols, the broader language of experience is harder for him to convey, but desire, on the other hand, is direct. We can ask him if he wants something and get an answer. Shortly after we started using the yes/no card, we discovered its potent simplicity, that if we're sitting in a restaurant, for instance, and found we've forgotten to pack his cards, we can generate a communication device simply by writing yes/no on a paper napkin. And so, black and white became another way in, or rather another way out.

He has his yes/no sign in front of him on the kitchen table. Just his presence at the table is a communication—he wants to eat, though he's had a cold the last few days and has not had much of an appetite. He ignores the food symbols on his plastic board, and having the yes/no card instead means he wants to play the question-and-answer game. So I pull items from the fridge, hold up yogurt, pudding, and cheese. Each one gets an emphatic tap on the *no*. *Do you want bread?* I ask. *Yes.* I pull out the peanut butter and the honey. He says *no* to both. I point to the toaster, *Do you want toast? Yes.* I get the butter and hold it up. Another *yes*. So I make the toast while he waits at the table, watching me. I butter it and cut it into squares, put the plate on the table, and drag out the exchange as long as possible: *Do you want this? Yes.* And I set it down. He slides the plate slowly and carefully toward him as if it's something he's afraid of waking, and then picks up a piece of the toast.

He doesn't even taste it. He raises his arm as high as he can and tosses the piece across the kitchen. I tell him to pick it up, and he shuffles over to get it and deposits it in the garbage can. Then he picks up his twirly dolphin by the twisty fins and carries it out to the living room. I can see that he is satisfied, that all he really wanted was a conversation and this is the best he can do.

I've sometimes wondered if when he stopped speaking and signing, he could have been making, in some way, a choice, even as some of the forces acting upon him were well beyond his control. Maybe communicating through walls had begun to wear on him and the development of a physical vocabulary, including some hitting and kicking, was inevitable, and the sitting on the ground with his legs crossed, arms folded, immovable as granite. It's nearly impossible to force an agenda on him then, the notion that he needs to go somewhere, get up, get moving, get to bed. Imagine the countless times a day when his plans are undermined by someone else's, when he's unable to make an argument that will convince, when the people around him encroach on the *him* of him.

The Ice

In his hut, Byrd is lying in his sleeping bag, trying to sort out who and where he is. His memory is a tangle of threads with nothing concrete at the ends until suddenly he remembers his routine. Even in the opening and closing of consciousness, the demands of his clocks, which have to be wound, and the sheets of the wind register and thermograph, which need to be changed, are tyrant enough to rouse him. Or so he understands later when he sees that the clocks are still going and the sheets, if two hours late, were changed though he won't remember doing it.

When he opens his eyes, he sees an enclosing dark and thinks that he has gone blind before realizing that his lantern is simply out of fuel and he is only, in very dim light, facing the wall.

And it's there against the wall, he writes, with the relief of being able to turn away from it, that he finds the parallel: he had brought similar relief once to his closest friend, Floyd Bennett. (Bennett had been with him when Byrd had made his attempt to be the first to fly to the North Pole; it was a trip that would, over the years, collapse Byrd's reputation. Alongside the acclaim and the tickertape parade, murmurings had begun to breed: he hadn't done it, the plane wasn't fast enough to reach the Pole in the time indicated, the recording of flight data had been twisted to support a fantasy. So said one faction. The rebuttal was never satisfactory.) In 1927, Bennett and Byrd were on a test flight of a Fokker airplane with its creator, Tony Fokker, at the controls when the plane went down. Fokker escaped out the emergency exit and Byrd found himself groping through the wreckage with a broken arm to where Bennett was held upside down, imprisoned but alive. Byrd sat with him while rescue was coming. *I'm done for*, Bennett said quietly. *I can't see anything*.

There was a slick of oil across his face. Byrd reached out and wiped the mess away from Bennett's eyes. And the look that transformed Bennett's face was beautiful.

A year after the accident, Byrd was in the suite that the Biltmore Hotel had donated to him as a preparation headquarters for his first expedition to Antarctica, and in the midst of couriers, volunteers, provisions, and the last-minute begging of funds, he received the crushing news that Bennett, already weakened from the crash, had died of pneumonia.

Now Byrd is in his hut staring at a dark wall, and Bennett has been dead for a half dozen years, but even if he were alive, it would make little difference. Anyone who can comfort Byrd, whether dead or alive, exists in a place far from here, and the only presence on the Barrier are the ghosts who, he'll later write, will push their thumbs into his eyes in the midst of a blizzard. He is utterly alone.

*

When Gabriel comes off the bus at the end of his school day, he presses hands sometimes with his aide as he's stepping down and then breaks into his loping run to cross the lawn and enter the house. He has, I know, so much to say. I can sense how the day has gathered around him, remnants of everything that has happened and everyone who has interacted with him are still clinging. The fire drills and music classes and the smells of the lunchroom. When he first started public elementary school, where he was fully included in the standard program until he was ten, the other students made an immediate connection with him, as if they knew he was more interesting than simply withdrawn and disabled, and could be gradually pulled out. Somehow they knew he was a boy who had a great belly laugh and sense of curiosity, someone who was actually fun, and they went to work on him in an effortless way, offering no apologies for crowding him. When he would push them away, they laughingly nudged him back and he didn't mind; they touched him until he was touchable. They taught him to revel in the swings and slides on the playground (squeezing in beside him at the top of the slide so he never had to ride down alone), and they modified their ballgames to include him. And what struck me about the games that I witnessed was how blithely the modifications were made, compared to the grown-up approach to inclusion, which involves so much brainstorming and head scratching. Without knowing it, they provided for him an enveloping and consistent sensory therapy, probably the best he has had. The elementary school provided a special room for him, complete with a little trampoline for his bouncing, for the occasions when he needed sensory breaks because he had begun to shriek or hit or for the delivery of therapeutic services, and the children painted on the walls for him, in huge letters, slogans like *Gabe Rules*.

By the time he was nine, his behaviors became more complicated, and now he spends much of his day in a self-contained room for students with special needs, but nevertheless when I open his backpack at the end of the day, I often find the drawings and notes that his typical peers make for him on a regular basis. His teacher helped him make a card for a boy who dotes on him, and the boy's response was a scrawled note: *Thank you for the card. I almost cryed I really appresheate it thank you again.* Another says, *Gabe you're the best! I hope you know that.* The girl who wrote it also drew pictures of a piano, sax, trumpet, and drums.

So his day has unfolded with affection and various therapies and yes-and-no questions and his daily peanut butter and jam sandwich. I read his teacher's note to find out some of the concrete details, always wishing there were more; finding out the rest of his daily story is a trading of nuance. He sits on the stairs in the hallway and I help him take his shoes off. Sometimes he reaches up and strokes my face or cups it in his hands. The day is all there, all of its boredom and excitement and color. We talk in our code. But occasionally when he gets home from school and sits on the stairs, it's something else that happens. His face will curl into the start of a cry, a mystifying, unfolding sadness, and he can't explain to me why.

It was actually the screaming that did it, not the throwing. The throwing—even though it was, and is, confounding—and the other reprises, cycles, and iterations were small compared to the shrieking. I read online another parent use the term *hyper-laughing*, although much too late. At the time, I thought R and I were witnessing something singular, though I should have known there is no such thing. There must be an attractive quality to the two-year cycle, because we experienced in the shrieking another instance of it, two years that culminated in a denouement, although this one was somewhat different from the lamp. The shrieking, which began when he was a preschooler, made us tight as guy wires. The episodes now are vastly reduced in frequency, but each one is still startlingly the same: the wild grinning and bouncing, followed by laughing that turns into a shriek at so high a decibel we've never been able to figure out how he can stand it. Our guess is that the vibration in his skull satisfies him, or distracts him from some other discomfort, or that the impulse simply has to be answered, regardless of how it feels. The more he screams and bounces, the more lost he is.

Here in the night, a shrieking episode gains power, becomes eviscerating. For R and me, the urge in the dark is to avoid coming completely apart, but the chronic lack of sleep has had its toll. Still, when I look back at the worst of the shrieking, I'm not sure how we survived it. S never mentions it, not even when the sounds turn up in the night and the house rumbles with the bouncing.

When Gabriel was about six years old, it was the screaming, and not the throwing, that made us place a call. It was the screaming that finally showed us he was unlike any child with Down syndrome that we knew. We contacted a Dr. P in Providence who specialized in people with Down syndrome. I had my own pet theory at the time, which is that I thought perhaps Gabriel had Tourette's syndrome, and that this explained his repetitions, his bouncing, his vocalizations; and it just so happened that when doing some research, I'd found a paper on the appearance of Tourette's syndrome in people with Down syndrome written by this exact Dr. P.

But Dr. P didn't think that Gabriel had Tourette's syndrome. After asking us a long list of questions, which he had to do in and around the shrieking, he sat quietly as Gabriel made a perfect display of the tortured waves that engulf him, showing how he disappears behind them. It was awful and wonderful, in a way; he didn't hold a thing back, it was all there for Dr. P to observe. I can only imagine how our family appeared to him, how ragged and limp, how confused that Gabriel's words had disappeared and that this was what had shown up in their place. Little did we know that Dr. P had, in fact, seen this before.

He studied R and me over the rims of his glasses. *I think your son is autistic*, he said.

There, the word plucked and pinned in the air. Autistic. It's not that I hadn't considered it; I had refused it. Time performed that hesitating trick, a crevasse opened, and R and I dangled there soundlessly, sledge dogs and all. Dr. P peered at us down the long slope of ice and offered, *I'll send you to someone else to confirm the diagnosis.*

R looked pale and grave. I felt a burst of rage form in my chest, even as I knew he was right.

Dr. P was gentle. He had had a son with Down syndrome who died suddenly at the age of thirty-three while the two of them had been attending a conference. Dr. P went on only hours later to give his talk, telling the audience . . . *there is a goodness, kindheartedness, humanity, and magic in our children that must be protected and never be betrayed.* He could see that I was struggling with the new word *autism*, with my anger. *Yes, I'm quite sure he is autistic,* he said. Gabriel screamed again, and no one reacted. We all pretended that our insides were not ringing with the sound.

When R and I left the doctor's office holding Gabriel's hands and he had quieted down now that he had proved who he was, we found an April day with pink and white petals covering the sidewalks and parked cars, and a light breeze. We got into the car and buckled Gabriel into his seat, and before R even started the engine, we looked at each other and started to laugh. Really laugh. I'm not sure we understood why, since this autism thing was veryverygrave andserious, and not, as they say, a laughing matter; it could have had a genesis similar to my grandmother's funeral when my sister and I started giggling—not because anything about it was remotely funny, but because sometimes the momentous begs the tragic and the mind will grab for absurdity instead. I think there was something else, also, having to do with language itself—now we had the word for *why*.

We did take Gabriel to be examined by a psychiatrist, a very experienced one who was at the end of her career and who, like Dr. P, had seen everything there was to see of the syndromes that can collect in the net of a single child. Hers was another of the offices trapped in time. There was an L-shaped sofa that we sank into, cabinets and shelves filled with files and books all around us, and an assortment of toys that S, who had come along, became absorbed in while the doctor held a thick file on her lap and watched Gabriel. He sat between R and me and took in his surroundings as he does, which is to say peripherally. I have wondered what he thinks at these moments, when he is being assessed and observed, when the doctor asks him questions and he tilts his head slightly in response. As he sat on Dr. M's sofa, he looked as though this scene was in keeping with his expectations, and I took that to mean that we had come to the right place. Perhaps a couple of weeks had passed between the time of Dr. P's assessment and this one, and I had grown used to the idea of autism in that short period. As Dr.

M observed Gabriel and took extensive notes about his development, going back in time to gestation, we were really progressing
to a truth I had known all along, that his autism was as old as he
was, that it had accompanied us all this way, unacknowledged but
nevertheless there. So much there in fact that its cumulative effect seemed greater than that of Down syndrome. In the realm of
brainstorms, it was, within Gabriel, a more potent system. Some
parents of children on the spectrum have told me how limiting
they find the diagnosis, that the act of naming the mystery doesn't
bring enlightenment or relief and instead can mean that their child
is rigidly perceived by other people, especially school staff. When
Dr. M confirmed Gabriel's autism, however, my response was the
antithesis of what I'd experienced when Dr. P first gave the diagnosis; this time I was accepting. Before we knew what to call it, autism
had actually felt more dangerous. Now it was quieter, smaller. Still a
gyre with a wide-open eye, but the storm had a name.

Gabriel was already receiving the therapies and communication aids that are normally applied to autism and that have never
been denied us (a perk of significant and obvious need is that you
rarely need to argue over it), but she had one thing to add: a medication to treat his physical and vocal tics, in the hope of reducing
the frequency of his screaming. R and I, who had always used non-
invasive therapies for him, were conflicted. What we put into his
body was something I had obsessed over; he hadn't tasted processed
baby food, for instance, until he was fourteen months old when
we resorted to it on a camping trip. In the case of his shrieking,
and leaving decibels aside, how do you decide what is legitimate
communication and what is an affliction? His right to make the
sound had to be weighed with his right to be freed from it. Here

is the thing of this odyssey: we are so often having to confront our preconceptions. Treating his seizures with medication had been an easy decision, or no decision at all actually—it was a given. But the specificity of treating his screaming—the screaming that seemed both of him and not of him—moved into that quagmire of children, drugs, and psychological disorders.

Except for this: we were witness to both the sound and Gabriel. It seemed like magical thinking to be offered a pill to ameliorate a sound—one that held the place where speech had stood—but there it was, and almost unbelievably, a low dose of it, called guanfacine, worked to some extent. Or rather, used in conjunction with nutritional and behavioral therapies, it works some of the time, lessening the severity. When his bouts of shrieking and bouncing sometimes still turn up in the night, which occurs much less often than it once did, we're reminded of their acuteness, how they fragment the night, but in our experience of autism, one thing is always relative to another. Sometimes the feat of simply managing can indicate, in some way, a comparative success. What I can say about the sound is that there is less of it and more of Gabriel.

The Ice

The Ice books that come to the house usually mention Ernest Shackleton. In 1914, on his third trip to the Antarctic, his expedition turned dark when one of his two ships, the sturdy *Endurance*, became trapped in the pack ice of the Weddell Sea and was slowly pressed to death.* The photographs show her turning brittle, turning into a ghost, her rigging a web of crystallized threads. She looks massive and fragile at the same time. After many months of being held by the ice and battered by the undulating pressure of its grip, she was approached by a group of emperor penguins who, lured by the sounds of the fracture, stopped to watch. About ten of them were gathered there and they made a strange, collective cry, prompting one of the men to say, *Do you hear that? We'll none of us get back to our homes again.*

Home. The specter of the place we're always shooting for, the nebulous point Shackleton and his men put at such a terrible distance that penguins came to cry. *Home* consists of what we think we're entitled to, what we were born to, and all we want is to get back to it. The irony is lost in the night but not the desire or the fear that we'll never find the way; those stick our eyelids open so we can continue scanning the dark for the shapes we don't recognize.

When Shackleton and his men, who had continued to live on the ship, finally sensed its inevitable demise, they raided her for essential items and set up camp on the ice. Shackleton ordered the men to give up anything unnecessary to survival and made a show of ripping some pages from his own Bible, the one given to him by Queen Alexandra, for keeping; he placed the Bible on the pile

---

* The other ship, the *Aurora*, moored at Ross Island, on the other side of Antarctica, also became trapped in the pack, drifting 700 miles away from the ten men who were left stranded on the Ice; three of the ten men perished, and the remainder survived 199 days before rescue.

of redundant items that the snow was claiming. Fresh words were another thing, however, and the men with diaries were allowed to keep them.

There is this, too: they had a radio receiver with them, meant to pick up Morse code broadcast from the distant Falkland Islands at the start of each month. They tuned in and waited, none of them expecting much, as the receiver strained for radio waves in the cold air and all they heard was static.

Three more weeks of suspension, the ice pressing hard on the ship, when suddenly Shackleton glimpsed movement, and the *Endurance* tipped, raising her stern. She gave in, and the ice, resolute as any predator, gulped her down. When Shackleton went to record the event in his diary, there was only the open sprawl of the page. He was able to leave just one sentence:

I cannot write about it.

After that, much hauling and clawing to keep alive. Shackleton and his companions sailed the wild sea in three small boats saved from the *Endurance* and landed at Elephant Island. He chose five men to accompany him further in one of the boats, the *James Caird*, just twenty feet long, to attempt at reaching South Georgia Island and its whaling station, a crossing of 800 miles. The remaining men waited on Elephant Island, using the other two boats, overturned, as sleeping quarters. The *James Caird* reached South Georgia after approximately sixteen days, and Shackleton continued over land with two of the men to find civilization at Stromness, which lay on the other side of seemingly impossible terrain. After finding the station manager and declaring who he was, Shackleton set in motion the necessary rescues. First, to collect the three men waiting on the other side of South Georgia, and then after five months and two aborted rescue attempts, he obtained an old steel-hulled boat from the Chilean government and found his men on Elephant Island. All this, and not a single casualty. Each of the men who originally had been on the *Endurance* got to go home.

provisions

On the other side of the Newport bridge, a band is playing jazz. Crossing the bridge is like crossing over. Gabriel dozes in the backseat of the car as he and I drive through the dark, from streets rimmed in farmland, south to the squat bridge that leads to Jamestown, to the Pell bridge with its cathedral arches and strings of lights and the quiet black sea underneath. It's quiet, too, in the car. I shut off the music as we coast along the bridge, under arches, toward the little club that waits. Gabriel's eyes flutter open—he knows we're getting close. Back at the house, I tied his shoes as he sat on the stairs and told him where we were going, that he would be hearing jazz, and he smiled, then galloped to the car, twirling one arm like a pinwheel, which he does when he tries to speed up. On the other side of the Newport bridge, his language is being spoken.

The guitarist says they are going to do "Summertime," and a guy who has been waiting to join in springs up from a bench near the street window. The musicians waiting to be called usually have a trumpet or sax, or something more exotic like a djembe, but this guy just has his voice and a mic. They start in on an upbeat, peppery version, very different from the languorous original but it's there, "Summertime," and I look at Gabriel, how he hugs the notes and presses into the grooves. This particular song belongs to his birth. After he was born and being cared for in the special care nursery, where he was hooked to machines and glassed in, I was alone in a room down the hall from him. I had the curtains drawn and the lights off when a cleaning woman stepped into the room and stirred the light of the open door with her broom. While she worked, she sang *Summertime and the living is easy*, the entire song as she swept the room and emptied the garbage can. *Your daddy's rich and your ma is good lookin'*. At the time, the duet with Armstrong and Fitzgerald was one of my favorite tunes, and it seemed like a gift that she sang it. *Hush little baby, don't you cry*. She left and I was supposed to be resting but, even after a couple of hours, sleep was impossible. R and I hadn't been able to get hold of most of our friends and relatives earlier in the day—this was in the days before smartphones, and we had called people on the phone beside my hospital bed to say that Gabriel was here. The following day would bring a chorus of responses, but that day, the day he was born, the voices were uncannily absent and it was as if the world had turned away. The nurses told me to grieve, ostensibly for the child that didn't turn up but, like sleeping, this also seemed impossible. There was no grieving for me to do, and as anxious as I was because he was in the intensive care unit, the moment of my hesitation had long passed and something else was settling in. I realized I was deeply in love, in a matter of hours, with my new son. It was past midnight, and I got up from the bed, moving my sore body carefully, and emerged into the light of the nurses' station where one of them sighed, *We can't seem to keep you down*. I walked past them and went to sit in a chair beside Gabriel in his incubator and watch him, so small and powerful.

So this version of "Summertime," the one he and I are listening to in the club, the one with the guy planting his feet deep in the ground while singing, is different than the usual meandering kind. It has a fast tempo and a raucous band turning the whole thing on its head. It gets more and more celebratory, and louder. There is no room for grief here and no cause. The drums are pounding. I lean toward Gabriel and tell him, *This one is yours*. I don't know if he can hear me, but it hardly matters; he is inside it.

It's time to take him home, head back through the night and over the bridge. The band has stopped playing, they're taking a break, and suddenly what has been stable becomes brittle for Gabriel. The musicians are ordering drinks and talking, heading for the back, or checking their instruments; they're standing on the curb with their cell phones. In the pause that forms, the desultory rushes in. And maybe that's it: Gabriel becomes aware of the irritating blandness and unpredictability of the everyday, the things that are happening when jazz isn't. I imagine he contends with his bodily sensations— the way his shoes feel, or the skin on his hands—at the same time that he seems to become aware of what is around him—a row of glasses on the bar, someone saying *jimmyheyman* and *shitnofoolin*, a dollar bill that catches in the draft from the door and flits to the ground like a giant moth, a woman's orange blossom perfume. I have tried to imagine what happens for him, something like a progression of notes: the voices, the shrill laughter, the siren out on the street, and most of all, the absence of jazz.

I am thirty feet away from him, wedged in between people at the bar to pay our bill, and when I glance over at him, I can see that it's beginning to happen: the opening of that secret world. *Do you belong to a secret society?* The signal isn't like crying or a crumpling face; instead, his eyes flash and he begins to bounce, first a little and then more, and then he starts to laugh and shriek, his expression suddenly vacant. There is no stopping the tempest once it starts, and whatever connections he has formed with other people and the music are lost. As I hurriedly pay the waitress, a man goes up to him and puts his hands out so Gabriel can give him a high five, and I think, *Don't fire him up.* The space that I have to cross to get to him suddenly seems like the one in dreams, dark and dense. Gabriel clouts the guy merrily, once, then again, and the guy just laughs, and he does it again. A flurry of hands and shrieking. Heads turn and the whole place is beginning to see him coming apart. I finally reach him, apologize to the man, saying, *He needs some space*, and turn to grab our coats from the rack. In the seconds of doing so, it begins again, the guy teasing him and more flailing and shrieking. I suddenly hear myself hissing *Just-back-off-give-him-some-room!* and taste something like kerosene in my mouth. I grab Gabriel's arm and pull him toward the door while trying to put his jacket around him. He is so charged I can feel him almost shimmering. Night flies open in a buzz of streetlamps when we hit the sidewalk.

The car is quiet as we start over the bridge with its sequence of lights: sequins. Gabriel watches the night out the window and he's calm again, settled into his seat, and after a while makes a small chirping sound. *That's right, Gabe. You're all right.* Remorse courses through; I wish I had protected him. Home, all I want is to be home. The streetlights begin to disappear, and we go farther into the dark until we are the only car on the road.

4 a.m.

*

delirium

PROVISIONS FOR BYRD:

3 Tables

2 Folding Chairs

2 Mirrors (1 big)

1 calendar

3 small floor rugs

1 fire proof asbestos rug

3 aluminum buckets

2 wash basins

2 candle holders

1 corn broom

2 whisk brooms

1 Pyrene fire extinguisher & 3 fillers

5 Automatic bombs & 4 plain bombs

1 can lubricating oil

1 5-gal. can packed with toilet paper

400 paper napkins

paper clips

3 doz. pencils

1 box thumb tacks

1 box rubber bands

2 reams 20 lb. bond paper (1000 sheets)

scratch pads

second sheets

carbon paper

1 box Lux toilet soap (50 bars)

1 " laundry chips (20 boxes)

1 Thermos bottle

1 Thermos jug

2 decks playing cards

4 yrds. oil cloth

50 big filing envelopes

drawing paper

cook books

hand grip

Quill tooth picks

selection of books

selection of records

Phonograph and spare parts

When I open Byrd's book, he is having nightmares. Sleep eludes him, too, or otherwise comes with terrors. Pains stab his head, his body, and dizziness brings him to his knees when he attempts to climb his ladder to check the aurora. He notes the irony that extreme cold is not really what is undoing him, but carbon monoxide poisoning. His enemy has become just another element in the polar night that slinks and blinds and, moreover, is locked inside the hut with him. Ice climbs the walls at what he estimates is an inch a day. The aurora unravels with or without him.

He sleeps intermittently, performs his tasks methodically, as if in a slow-motion film. Desire no longer nudges at music or books—his phonograph takes too much energy to wind, and he can't concentrate on his reading—but grows within a rotation of other needs: faith, warmth and, especially, thirst. He's too weak for his usual ice retrieval and resorts to getting on the ground of his food tunnel, where his footsteps have loosened a trough of dirty snow, and pulls some into his bucket. He can't wait to melt it on the stove, so he heats it with alcohol tablets instead and drinks it down.

How the body deflects exactly what it has invited: he vomits. He tries again, convincing his body with very little sips, and returns to his sleeping bag. He makes the simple plea that has been my own on so many nights: he begs for sleep.

✳

When he is lucid, he records the day's actions as a defense against his increasingly gauzy memory. Tending to the thermograph and register, he is bitter and thinks, *Without me they could not last a day.* Between the scholars back in civilization and the night's wilderness, he is just a data collector taking the Barrier's pulse, even as it is costing him his life. The machines' rhythms have become emphatic—he cannot let them down; they connote being. He calls his thermograph and register resolute and faithful, also remorseless. His stove is a villain, and his bucket greedy. The flames of two red candles are—and here his tenderness is almost unbearable—friendly. Inside and out, the ice creeps and invades. The dark is an increasingly present companion, a houseguest he is afraid to repel with his lantern because it uses gasoline, but he lusts for light.

His appetite has been meager, but he eats a piece of chocolate (whatever explorers deem vital to survival in Antarctica, they never seem to fail to include chocolate) and an Eskimo biscuit before passing out again. When he comes to, it is as if during sleep he has been somewhere else, maybe home, and so he is newly confronted with his situation, wakes to see that he is still at a small table in a small hut on the enormous Barrier. He slumps forward, sobbing.

In Camus' version, Sisyphus, who has woken up to find himself in the underworld, convinces Pluto to let him make a brief return home under the pretense of having to chastise his wife and so Pluto lets him go. *But when he had seen again the face of this world, enjoyed water and sun, warm stones and the sea, he no longer wanted to go back to the infernal darkness.* Eventually, of course, he is hauled back to the underworld where his rock is waiting. He sheds his rebelliousness, turns forever to begin again, and, alongside scorn and resignation, he is said to experience something else; Camus leaves off with the line, *One must imagine Sisyphus happy.* It seems to me that when Byrd starts sobbing, he isn't just breaking down but actively rebelling because *the smiles of earth* are still with him—unlike Sisyphus, he retains hope of getting home.

Here in the comfort of my house, I can watch him in the intimacy of his hut, in the glow of the stove or some candles, as if his rebelling is not my own and I'm indifferent to him. But I'm not indifferent. The home I want to reach is the one where night has returned to its slippery, silvery self, where my child isn't governed so much by waking. I'm not indifferent to Byrd's suffering because I recognize it. I can almost reach out and touch him on the shoulder, as if to nudge him out of his nightmare. He is sobbing while fear consumes him at the thought of what will happen to his wife and children should he not make it out of this place. I know how his story ends, and I want to tell him that he'll be safe.

His sleeve freezes to a spot on the table where earlier he spilled some water, and after freeing his arm, he gets in his sleeping bag. Writing letters to his wife and children, he thinks of Scott's dying words, *Last entry. For God's sake, look after our people*, and places the letters in a green metal box that he stores on a shelf. Instructions to two of his men he ties to a nail that would normally suspend his lantern. Sleep comes and goes, as does a flickering of gratitude that he is still alive.

＊

He is awake and feeling lucid. He lets the beam of his flashlight linger on a bottle of sleeping pills, then takes the bottle and pours the contents into his hand. Sleep and death, perhaps they are the same here. Like the snow crystals that surround him, the pills are white and minimal enough. They can be tamed in the hand, held on the tongue; they connect to a region of obliterating white. Taken collectively, they are a door.

There is an alternative, however: he sees a piece of blank paper lying on his bunk. It is another kind of portal. He writes on it,

The universe is not dead.

figment [no.2]

It is early spring and I'm running through wetlands from which
the color has been drained. Trees are still bare, and the ones in the
middle of the marsh spike up headless and limbless. But activity
under the water's surface belies what appears on top to be a still
frozen quiet; everything is actively becoming something else. Tufts
of grass burst up among the dead leaves. The trees farther along the
trail, where the marsh isn't digesting them, are alive and bud-cov-
ered. Several days of rain have soaked the bark through, soaked
everything so that the forest is black.

My feet hitting a small wooden bridge cause a great egret to
burst out of the trees. The scene unlocks suddenly, the black trees
snapping out this flag of white. The sky is a slope of white, too,
banked and solid, into which the egret vanishes.

The door's the thing. Gabriel opens the night with it, pounds on it, and the sound is like a giant wanting in. His bedroom door shudders and the sound comes for me, as if the giant is there in my ear. The pounding wrecks the heart. If R and I have been in a deep sleep, we feel the burst of adrenaline, start panting before our feet hit the floor. If R is the one answering the terrible drum, he'll remember it in the morning; if I'm the one to get up, he'll go back to sleep within seconds and in the morning will often remember nothing about the giant in the night.

When Gabriel gets out of bed, he'll sit on the floor behind the door with his legs straight out in front of him. He's so flexible that when drowsy enough, he'll simply fold his torso down to rest between his legs, his cheek against the floor, and has been known to sleep in this position for several hours. His legs have begun to turn outwards from so many sessions of sleeping this way that we try as much as possible to get him back into bed and lying prone. If he's sitting on the floor and doesn't fold himself and go to sleep, but instead sits there and wonders what to do, well, there is the door.

In the metaphysics of autism, doors have significance for him. He bangs them, drums his fingers on them, runs his nails lightly along them, pounds them so the hollow interiors of the cheap ones fill with sound. (He has been given actual drums, but he doesn't engage them the same way.) He pulls and yanks and thrusts them, and his favorite: he slams. He swings them open wide before the push, so they fly shut, look like wings in midflap. The door in the night is his communication device, his conduit and sounding board, a tribal drum signaling haste, come running—now. Listen to Philly Joe Jones on the drums at the start of the Bill Evans Trio's "Night and Day"; it is the sound of Gabriel playing his door.

He has been fascinated with doors since toddlerhood, perhaps because of their binary open and shut, or maybe because of their potential to reveal. Of a wall, but not a wall. There are keys and codes and passwords, letter slots and numbers, welcome mats or, in cartoons anyway, trapdoors. The space on the other side could be a brick wall or infinity. The door is glass, or has a window, or is nothing more than a veil or beaded strings. There are doorbells that glow, and brass knockers shaped like a pear or a face. Doors can be whispered open or broken down. Maybe that's the thing he wants most when he's pounding: the way out. It's not as simple as it would seem. The boy who can fall inside jazz and find his way home again finds a doorknob hard to operate, so perhaps this is part of the draw. A child's development, I've discovered, isn't the linear progression some would have you believe; there are detours, blind alleys, rotaries. He can use a spoon, create his I-wants, and work the buttons on his portable DVD player, but doorknobs, pencils, and shoelaces confound him. Even covering himself with his blanket once he gets back into bed is a kind of motor planning that stalls him.

When I open his door, he looks up at me with an alert gaze from his spot on the floor. He gets to his feet and plunges onto his bed. I tuck him in, turn out his light, draw the door shut behind me as I leave. I wonder what he dreams about, what his nightmares are like. A dim light glows from the bathroom, and my shadow glides briefly along the wall.

Pounding on the door is another way of talking; he collects ways of saying. Recently he discovered that the main phone unit attached to our kitchen wall has a speaker button on it and that if we aren't right around him but he wants us to be, he can press the button and summon us with a long, loud dial tone. Which is followed by two rings, and then a recording (which can be heard clearly upstairs) of an operator, *If you'd like to make a call, please hang up and try again. If you need help, hang up and then dial your operator.* Then the recording starts again before reverting to the dial tone. We've learned to materialize as fast as we can at the first sound of the tone, come running before the damn recording comes on again. We'll find him with his fingers clasped together over his belly and moving contentedly foot to foot.

He uses what he finds at hand to send out his messages. There is a night that I open his door to find that he has stripped his mattress. I have heard of children who do this on a regular basis, take apart all the blankets and sheets, and then go for the curtains, but this is the first time that I've seen him do it, and so I wonder if this is the start of a new obsession that will confound each and every attempt to be resolved, and what, in his code, it means. Each thing he does tends to come freighted with significance, or at least this is what I hope to find, even in his act of unmaking the bed. Is he trying for the simplicity of the mattress or the chaos of the blanket heap? Imitating his parents changing the sheets or just reveling in coming apart?

But, remarkably, he doesn't leave the mattress empty. He's placed five of his twirly-creatures in a line at the top of his bed. The pillow is on the floor with the blankets. He sits on his bare mattress, looking at the animals as if they are an audience. He has gathered a committee, a crew, or witnesses. Despite the hour and the bed's state, this dismantling is good news. He has rarely engaged in what is considered imaginative play, and this looks for all the world like playing.

Perhaps the twirlies know his secrets, or he theirs. They are expressions of the material world's mystery and its dissonance, its sheer weirdness, as if they're jokes about beingness. They are studies. His favorites include a small pink pig, a zebra, a duck, and a tiny bear wearing a jester's cap. Each one has been given to him by a friend or relative who no longer knows what to get for him, and each has been exhausted to the point of coming apart, the fur matted, the eyes gone, and in the case of the bear, the paws have been clutched into oblivion and the jester's cap is now just a small velvet shred. They have been tortured beyond reason and still they won't tell.

I know other children with variants of autism whose material obsessions yield similar specificity. In J's case, he is passionate about empty but fragrant paper coffee cups or Altoids tins. In H's case, he has a small toy aquarium with fish that swim when he presses a button, and which he carries with him everywhere. B's passion is a ragged bunny on a string and chicken nuggets. Each child is a connoisseur of their chosen object, which if no longer rewarding will be replaced by another, equally specific. It is not just any bear or fish or chicken nuggets, but very particular ones. I imagine that they are each constructing a roster of necessities, the ones that will snag their attention and hold off the dissonance within and around them. Something like a list of provisions.

✳

There is a tiny beach not far from my house where the water coughs up so many little white shells that they have to be shoveled back by tractors twice a year. Millions of small worlds, whorled homes, tombs. Footsteps make a crinkling sound and send dozens of tiny spiders shooting across the shells like brown darts. The Atlantic swells, becomes sea after sea until they swirl around the ice where Byrd is, was, one more facet of my connection to him. What is cerulean one day is gunmetal the next. The changeling water relentlessly folds, and where it meets the shore, it shapes and hammers the way it does around the islands and pack ice in Antarctica.

One of my favorite places to run curves along the ocean, and I can stand on the beach when I'm done and look at the bay, watch poised egrets stare hard into the surf for their catch. Across the Narragansett Bay is a tiny island where, on a day in July, a big band is playing. We cross to the island for the day, curl on a sunny, hot hill to sip sour lemonade and listen to the band. S, who is bored, sprawls on the grass and rolls repeatedly down the hill, but Gabriel sits on the blanket and listens. After the concert, we walk through the crowded streets and wonder about the people who live in the cottages year-round, think about them in the winter winds, crossing gray seas on the slow ferries, relishing the quiet when the tourists are huddled on the mainland. When we are hot and tired, we board the ferry to go back, and support Gabriel as he walks cautiously up the steep metal stairs.

We settle in and the boat fills with heat and people. Gabriel, tilting his head, watches a group who partied on the island. They are college age and lugging folding chairs and beer coolers. I photograph the sea through the water drops on the windows, and S asks for potato chips and more lemonade.

We are only about fifteen minutes from the mainland when a man comes to stand close to Gabriel. Too close, and Gabriel swats him. He has been calm until this point, has tucked in the urges that no doubt have been circulating through him like blood cells. I cover his hands with mine and apologize to the man, but when the man turns and looks at Gabriel, really sees his face, his expression changes. I've seen the transfiguration many times; a stranger comes upon Gabriel and receives him well or not, but anyway receives him.

Some people are wary of him and encounter their own darkness, but others seem to suddenly feel something sentimental and want to convey it. The man is stalled by his surprise and he says to Gabriel, and to me, *I'm sorry, I'm so sorry*. He bends his body unknowingly into that curve of autistic space that crackles like an electric fence around Gabriel, he steps into that static-filled space. *I'm sorry, I'm so sorry*. He lists with the boat, dazzled and maybe drunk, and is unable to stop staring at Gabriel or delivering his apologia. I struggle to keep Gabriel's hands from flying up into the man's face as I say, *It's okay, it's okay*, hoping to release him from Gabriel's orbit. He staggers finally into the crowd and vanishes. I sit back in my seat, look out past the people to the bit of sky showing in the windows.

I don't see Gabriel's hand rise up. The movement is so fierce and quick that I register only something like a molten red that appears before the pain, and the feeling of time slowing as my nose absorbs the hit in a way I would have said it couldn't accommodate. And so I cover my face with my hands, and I think, though it's not, that my nose is broken.

It isn't possible to think, not in the usual way. I know the ferry continues listing and the crowd, if it sees what has happened or not, continues to knit and unknit between the aisles and vinyl seats, and there must be sounds, but all is silence. Silence and the color red, and R's hands tight above my elbows, lifting me out of the seat and placing me in another one as I scurry into myself as far as possible. It's not Gabriel I want to shrink from but the gaze of the nearby strangers who will not realize the dark of the secret society that's just been revealed is only one aspect, and only one aspect of Gabriel, that the simplicity of the hit is bordered by the complexities of *saying*—so many years of him trying to say what he feels, what he wants, who he is. I want to tell them that if their words had drifted away, they too might find themselves lashing out after them. I want them to understand what is impossible to understand: I know how we got here.

Gabriel seems to retreat also, at least he appears to be doing so when I finally open my eyes again. The heat suffocates us, and the depleted air, and the silence, too, that folds like waves, one over the other.

The Ice

The looking glass hangs on a nail near a shelf and Byrd takes it down. It seems that he's ready to see himself as he really is, in this poorly lit place where the shadows transform what is already liminal. The face that appears in his shaving mirror, however, is folding with age and weakness, and shows the spots the cold has eaten. He's so disheartened by what he sees that he'll have to answer another bout of mental disintegration with visions of being surrounded by sunlight and the people he loves. The following afternoon he'll test his battery-powered radio and tune it to the weekly broadcast from Little America to the United States, so he can steady himself with distant voices. The men at Little America will tell the audience about the cows, named Klondike, Deerfoot, and Southern Girl, and the calf born on the journey named Iceberg, that were brought to the Ice to supply milk, how one of the cows won't lie down and another refuses to get up. Byrd's wife and children in Boston will have piled onto his bed at 9 Brimmer Street and tuned into the broadcast. The day after that, he'll have a radio schedule with his men where he'll stop himself from calling for help and he'll contrive messages in his inept code to make it appear that all is more or less well. But at the moment, he is suspended in his little mirror, watching himself watching himself; he is turning in the vortices that layer Antarctica, a witness to being consumed.

Gabriel rarely watches himself. He only catches glimpses. Like our cat, he'll often smoothly avert his gaze when he's standing in front of a mirror, not as if he's afraid to see himself but as if he has no curiosity about how he appears in the glass nor interest that there is a glass at all. Then again, maybe he understands the power of the other self, and like Byrd would prefer not to see the one that is darker and harder to grasp.

He discovered his shadow when he was two and a half and still fairly new to walking. He had a wide, uneasy stance and his hands out at his sides, swiping the air for balance. I had taken him to a neighborhood park, and he lurched over the grass toward the sand. Though he still had some of his words and signs, the long slow diaspora having only just begun, he was quiet and focusing his attention on the ground. When he reached the pale sand, the dark slice of him was sharpened and he stopped. Looked, moved. Looked. Moved again.

He stared at the ground, at the boy whose legs stretched like ribbons from his feet. He watched how the shadow mimicked, thinly but precisely, the aspect of the lit world that was him. He looked like he couldn't get over it.

✳

Byrd is late for radio contact with his men. Dyer, back at Little America, has been saying Byrd's call letters KFY and waiting for him to answer in his poor Morse code, which Dyer grows tired of doing and plays music instead. When Byrd finally gathers strength to run the generator and tune his receiver, he likes what he hears. He listens in the hut's dim light, surrounded by crystal walls, waiting for the music to finish before he'll key anything to let them know he's there. I think of him receiving the notes—a little like Gabriel listening to jazz, sitting, receiving the notes that have been able to travel the distance. One hundred and twenty-three miles lie between Byrd and the sounds' origin, not so far really, except that in this place the distance may as well be infinite. For tractors and men, the ice is full of spikes and razors, and crevasses that open to plunge downward for hundreds of feet. Byrd and his men could not be farther apart.

I picture him slumped there in a chair beside the receiver when he hears Charlie Murphy's voice:

Oversleep, Dick?

Maybe Byrd pauses here, takes a breath before tapping his code:

No.

Busy.

*

It's June 28 and Tom Poulter is sending his voice from Little America across the ice to Byrd's hut. He is making a proposal: that he and a few of the men come to the hut to observe meteors, and that

Byrd, if he wishes, could return with the tractor to Little America. The journey out to him, barring storms, crevasses, breakdowns, and navigational issues, would take a few days.

Since Byrd began disintegrating, there has been a dance between him and Poulter, one in which he tries to lead and then pulls back. His rough Morse code tangles his meaning, but he speaks in code, too, when he holds back how ill he's become, how sleepless, how he forces himself to eat. How he's dying. He thinks he's got Poulter and Murphy fooled, but because the messages scattering in from Advance Base show gaps and confusion, they have their suspicions. Instead of asking him directly if he needs rescue, which they know he would have to refuse because of the dangers involved and the lack of light on the Barrier, they have decided on this approach: a proposal. Meteor observation. What is, for their part, a rescue in disguise, planned for clear weather sometime between July 23rd and the 29th. In the fumes and cold of his hut, the idea elates him at the same time that it rocks him with remorse. He is a pendulum. Poulter's voice comes again in the hut, *Well, what do you think of it?* Byrd taps out *Wait a minute*, then tells him to make trial runs and let him know the results. After he signs off, he continues to mull and vacillate, long into the night.

He will write that these are *days of great beauty, shadowless days*, and he will write that *this damnable evenness is getting to me.*

He will go to the calendar that is hanging on his wall, and because it is the end of the month, he'll be about to turn over June like turning a page in a book: finished. Except that what he'll do is measure the outside dimensions of the calendar instead. As if, in his cube of ice within ice, separated by more ice and a rift in his soul from any other human being, his consolation is this precise assessment of time in its little blocks. Imagine the delicate measuring, like a tailor or a coffin fitter, the focused attention: twelve inches along one side and then fourteen along another. He measures with no reward other than to know the scale. He notices that in June he crossed off some days but left the others blank.

After this, his spirit lightens. He gains strength to crank his phonograph and create a food cache near his bunk in the event that he weakens enough that he can't get up.

He freezes an ear in his sleeping bag, and watches the ice climb the walls to within three feet of the ceiling. He sends a message to Little America, approving plans for their base-laying journey.

He reads *The House of Exile*.

*

The problem of getting into bed, feeling R's warmth and the blankets, is that the pleasure of it is painful, the idea of having to relinquish it again. Every sound is heightened, and I circle inside my vigilance, anticipate the click of Gabriel's light switch and his thump again onto the floor. There are times that I've heard a shriek or moan and staggered down the hall only to find him silent and sleeping and realize that I've dreamed the sound. Night is an amplifier, enlarging every vibration— the furnace turning off and on, hot air rushing in the vents, the metallic pings and ticks as the ducts adjust—as if each is worth being heard.

When Byrd talks about the sounds of the Barrier as it splits and shifts, it is as though he means the Barrier is trying to speak. The voice is like thunder but says nothing he can use. Words and sounds in his hut have been placed in containers—books, the phonograph, his radio receiver—but the containers are muffling bell jars, specimen cases. He receives language through a scrim and the result is mostly a diffusion of meaning. He is losing language.

*

R and I are so accustomed to Gabriel's sounds that when we hear something we can't identify, we're inclined to let it go uninvestigated, New England being a stormy place with no shortage of rumbling. One autumn night a wind gust came through, according to the National Weather Service, at 50 mph and took hold of a backyard poplar, waltzing it straight to the ground and finding the only clear vector between a fence, the garage, a large spruce, and some cedars. What we heard around 2 a.m. was something like a pot being scrubbed, a hundred matches struck, and furniture moved. It was easy, since it appeared to have nothing to do with the boys, to let its mystery go—it seemed best to stay snug rather than uncover something unpleasant. It didn't sound, for instance, like an entire tree lying down on the lawn. We forgot about it and slid back into sleep.

The next morning, R was munching his cereal when he suddenly remembered the sound and, looking out a back window, saw the problem. We put on our coats and went to stand by the base of the tree that was wrenched open, exposing blond plains of smooth wood. Like Gabriel watching his shadow, we couldn't seem to get over it. I tried to remember what the sound had been like, the sheer layers of rushing and collapsing, but I could barely hold onto it. Standing among the branches was entrancing, and I could see the rents in the ground, the craters that revealed an earlier violence where now there was only quiet. I thought about the force required to take a tree that had staggered for fifty years toward the sky and simply make it: stop.

But it wasn't the first time. There had been a winter storm when the boys were smaller, one that had snuffed out the lights and heat, and I'd bathed the boys by candlelight. I remember that I had a fever and when I looked out the bathroom window through the sheet of rain, I actually thought for just a moment that the small tree lying down across the snow wasn't really there. The black leafless branches were eerie and like an undeciphered script. When I turned away from the window and looked at Gabriel sitting in the tub and at the candles flickering, I wanted to explain the power outage to him, describe the invisible. The outside forces. I wondered how to give meaning to his waiting for the lights to come back on, how to tell him what is change and shift and light and dark, and what is waiting, even as I believed that somewhere inside him he already had them figured out. Especially waiting.

Fats Waller said that if you have to ask what jazz is, you'll never know.

The neighbors walked over to circle the poplar and wonder, and when we explored the cracked trunk, we found a fungus traveling inside it in white plumes. When we thought back to the tree before it fell, we realized it had been giving us signs in the form of dropped branches and a subtly elegant lean, but we all stared at the downed tree with our hands jammed in our pockets, having nothing to offer it but surprise. A tree is just a tree until it's sideways along the ground.

A boy is just a boy until his words disappear.

The Ice

Byrd has to rest on every other ladder rung when he goes topside for his observations, and eventually he is so weak that he simply approaches the polar night like a trapdoor spider, peeking out from a crack in the lid. A pain in his shoulder that he has been nursing worsens, along with the feeling that he's drugged. He watches the temperature on the Barrier and in his hut fall and hover. He will only allow himself to run the stove for a short time, resulting in a piece of meat, that sits on his table for five days, refusing to thaw. He vomits milk, reels with exhaustion, and still he fills out form no. 1083.

He writes, *This is habit carrying on, not you. You are through.*

provisions

Byrd is right: we can be half-dead and still resort to our habits. Sometimes the habit is the only thing that seems real, or reliable. At the very least, it is familiar. Maybe this is the thing that makes Sisyphus go. It is not just the gods that force him, but habit. He is so charged with his repetitions that he becomes the essence of the place that he's in.

There is a night when my eldest sister is visiting and sleeping in a room across from Gabriel's, and he has started laughing and shrieking shortly after midnight. He has never been quite as wild as this with a guest in the house and I feel panicked, wanting him to stop. I still want to hide just how bad this gets. The hours surge and rock like boats, his squeals traveling the house in bursts, the night in fragments again as I try to contain him (and in the morning my sister emerges, stunned at what has gone on because experiencing the sounds is different from hearing us mention them, and I say to her, even though this is old hat, *Welcome to autism . . .*). The small hours pass and dawn finally comes. At around 7 a.m. I crawl into bed beside R, who hasn't heard a thing. He wakes and, realizing that I've been up all night, wants to know why I didn't get him up, he would have taken over. But I don't know how to explain, how to say that Gabriel and the night have affected me, made me different; the molecules are still in my skin. I'm full of nebulas, dying stars, solar winds, and substorms. Night is in me.

Byrd is transmitting: *Ok here.*

OK, OK, OK.

But he is keying into the wild, blindly. Two days before, his gasoline-driven radio generator failed and he dismantled it so that it sprawled in bits across the table. Back when he was learning to fly and he had taken apart his first airplane engine, he had been amazed at how the components, loosened from their former whole, seemed dead. No matter how he aligns the radio generator parts, he cannot make them live. Now he is using the battery-powered unit, with its two handles for cranking, which he finds exhausting. There is a copper switch he can throw one way for transmitting and the other for receiving. His obligation to send his signals, as jumbled as they are, weighs on him, the fact that he is responsible for his men and that not hearing from him could cause them to come for him without proper planning. Days before, on July 5, he sent his signals over different frequencies but received only silence. At last, Dyer's voice sprinkled in, delighting him. Murphy came on and spoke about the journey out to him, how they were weighing the challenges and not to expect them until late in the month. Byrd felt the discomfort that he'd given himself away, that despite knowing how treacherous the journey would be, they were going to do it anyway, because of him; and he reveled in the hope that he might get out of this place alive.

*

As morning gets closer, I start to feel more urgent. Maybe this is the most difficult time because night is almost over and I'll have to officially get up and start the day. I'm not as sanguine as Camus claims Sisyphus to be. The begin-again is the most difficult part, anticipating it, feeling the opportunities for sleep that haven't even arrived already slip away. This is the hour that I have sat and wept, not for Gabriel's words (communication, he's shown me, is broad) or fear of the future or even parental guilt but for the simple lack of sleep. Not every night has to be tackled in fragments, hour by hour, but most of them do, so that insomnolence has made it hard to grasp the one thing that energizes me regardless of day or night, which is meaning. I want the damn meaning, and it's become difficult to see. Without a clear head, there is very little that makes sense. Like Cherry-Garrard, I've begun to think that what I would give for a good night's sleep is five years of my life. But I don't mean it.

The Ice

Byrd has his first bath in a week and seeing that his skin hangs, estimates he's lost perhaps fifty-five pounds in total since he came to Antarctica. It is Monday, July 9, and he signals into the night, trying to snag a response from his men, but nothing comes. Tuesday, again: nothing. He undoes the radio receiver and transmitter, unwinds them into their meaningless parts trying to find a problem he can amend; then reassembles the parts into beings that will reveal in the silence the presence of other people. And still: nothing.

His lust for light is so strong that, damning the fumes, he lights his pressure lantern and bathes in what he imagines is coming from the sun. The sun, which is stalling out of sight before swinging back for the south now that the Winter Solstice has occurred.

He combs the night for sounds, but nothing again until Dyer's voice is there in the hut, a ghost-voice, and he keys back frantic:

Heard you. Have had radio trouble. Come in.

And as he keys the words, he says them aloud, even though there is no one who can hear him.

✳

Back at Little America, the continuity of the polar night has led to entropy. The men's repeated bacchanals have forced Poulter to hide the liquor supply, moving it from one location to another, then another, before he surreptitiously empties the bottles into the Barrier. The men respond by draining the alcohol from compasses and pouring mouthwash through a homemade still. In their off-hours, they push steel rods into the snow, trying to divine the location of the missing liquor.

This is how the dark and the cold have played them. Some of them no longer believe in an edifying Antarctic mission. They accuse Byrd of various black arts: abandonments, ego trips, self-serving agendas. And when Poulter and Murphy argue for an early venture to retrieve Byrd, some argue against. They don't know the extent to which Byrd has disintegrated because the information has been kept from them; what they do know is that his original orders, given when he left for his sojourn, stated that no one should come for him until light was on the Barrier. It would seem to them that the man needing rescue should indicate clearly that he needs it. Byrd will later write that *the caves at Little America seethed with dissension*. He didn't know the half of it.

The arguments carry on until a vote is taken. After Poulter and Murphy narrowly win their case, a night watchman sees something out on the ice. A figure, dressed in furs, is discovered facedown in the snow. It would seem that Byrd has stumbled in from the Barrier and collapsed. Stumbled in from 123 miles away, having navigated blindly from one speck on the ice to another speck, in the dark, through walls of wind and crystals. And yet, in night's logic, it appears that he is there and so some of the men descend on the figure, haul him inside, all the while believing it's Byrd until they try to revive him and discover it's one of their own who has been playing a joke.

Just joking.

Byrd doesn't know any of this. I wonder if anyone ever tells him how a terrible joke was played, one in which he got his wish. Somehow, he has desired hard enough that another Byrd is born, a doppelganger that navigates the void and is lifted from the ice by numerous hands, finds freedom.

*

So I have wondered what *he* means, what is signified by Gabriel, even as I know the answer is really the question. The labels attributed to him, and the insistence of other people on keeping him in step with his designations, is far beyond the point, and yet I've rummaged the labels for a lost document, a sacred text with the thought that maybe the answer is inside what we say that he is. Even as I know better.

When Gabriel was about four years old, one of his eyes turned in, a strabismus due to farsightedness, so his ophthalmologist wrote a prescription for glasses. A burr was in my stomach as I wondered how we would convince the one who was inconvincible to place something on his face and keep it there. R and I joked darkly about staples. We fretted that if he rejected the glasses his ability to interact and to learn would be further compromised. We knew enough to pick a moment to introduce them when he was standing in front of the television, watching his favorite episode of *Bear in the Big Blue House*, so that once the glasses were perched on his nose, Bear was suddenly clear to him. It was as smooth as that, and he wore them well for a few years until his farsightedness corrected itself and the glasses were no longer needed.

But it was picking up the glasses from the optical store in the first place that was a seminal moment in the meaning of labels. R and Gabriel and I went together to the store, which was tightly serene. Layers of glass and mirrors on desks where customers leaned in to be fitted, a quiet carpet, and wood pillars. R and Gabriel didn't go in but stayed on the sidewalk, Gabriel walking ahead of his father. Back and forth. I sat inside, on one of the chairs along the wall as I waited to pick up our order, and there was a woman seated nearby. Various customers were choosing frames or waiting to pay. The woman watched the window where Gabriel and R went by in one direction and then turned and went in the other. The woman announced, *There's a little boy with Down syndrome.* Just that. Her friend was standing nearby and widened her eyes to signal that the mother was sitting right there, but the woman who spoke didn't understand. The room was crackling and I seemed nearly invisible. *There's a little boy with Down syndrome.* She had said so, and it meant something. Was it like seeing a rare bird and letting the other birders know—or was it more like a car crash? A boy! With Down syndrome! He had entered, been objectified as small talk, and I wondered if she would mention him that night at dinner. I felt like I was watching people undress, like I was spying on a world I was no longer privy to. I had had my suspicions that maybe these small pronouncements were what happened when I wasn't in earshot; as the parent, I had been subject to different kinds of remarks. (If you want to burn the britches of a mother of a child with special needs, tell her that God only gives special children to special people. Yes, it's true. In the most secret parts of the secret society, this is viewed as probably the most condescending aphorism there is, even as it's made poster-sized or written on a coffee mug. We'll nod and smile when someone inflicts it, and then some of us will go home to smash things.) I often wondered at what point people realized his difference, because in those days, when he was still a preschooler, the characteristics were occasionally less clear, he could shape shift. His autism and his darkness were, and are, invisible to the passing gaze. But she had seen, and I wanted to know the secret. There is a boy with Down syndrome, and then what?

I was irritated by the woman who knew my identity and was trying to give me away. I wanted to be, if only for a moment, not his mother, not his other, but one of the people inside the shop (because I wasn't one of them, not really, and this was, after all, a shop of seeing). But it would seem that the ones in the shop were not in a better position than I, just a different one. As this woman was snagged on Gabriel's difference, so was I fascinated by hers.

If there was more, it wasn't said; the woman who had spoken looked uneasily at me and knew.

Four years later, a woman who was a social worker employed by Gabriel's school came to the house with a brimming satchel of papers and books. Gabriel was mysterious enough and delayed enough that she came to fill out an assessment about his development, which would be filed with the school district in order that he would continue to receive appropriate services. In other words, he had to be categorized. Assessments like these are a periodic occurrence in the realm of special needs, which is nothing if not well documented, and services often depend on them. Where the child falls in relation to every other child is probed and charted and filed. Gabriel confounds the usual tests (which might require the child with special needs to give verbal responses or to complete puzzles and games), and even the ingenious ones developed for children exactly like him. He was an uncharted coastline, and so she had to rely on me to draw him out on paper.

We sat at the kitchen table and she filled the surface with forms and white binders that she rummaged through for various slips of paper, the metal rings snapping and unsnapping like tiny bear traps. She used a black pen to make a few notes, the satchel sagging like a giant toad on the floor by her feet. It appeared to be gulping not just reams of paper but some toys, too. The toys in these circumstances are never just toys, but tests. She took a long hit of the coffee I'd made for her while she read a form.

She asked about his birth (philosophically complex), other diagnoses (how long is the form?), where we've lived (Canada and the US), how he slept (oh my), what was his favorite color (R and I, feeling fraudulent, have sometimes picked blue when asked this), what he liked to eat (most things). We combed through the developmental milestones of the past years, tabulating and calculating. It was difficult, it seemed, to add him up. Typical child development filled a chart with age-markers down the sides, the kind of thing that gives parents of children with autism, for instance, chills. You know that the number of children, with or without disabilities, that fall within the confines of the chart is in the many millions and yet your particular child floats in an unmarked area somewhere out on the tabletop, where there's a jam smear and some crumbs.

At one time in our house, the charts and the ideas that belonged to them enjoyed incredible power. The going theory, which is still going in many parts, was that the brain had something like a time-limited plasticity and had to be stuffed with as much information as possible before the age of five or six, after which it was considered too late. If the child was left staring off into space at age seven, it was likely caused by insufficient effort on the part of the surrounding adults, the ones responsible for packing the brain. That the learning process was more flexible than the current paradigm was left unconsidered in favor of unquestioned, panic-inducing timelines—after all, nobody wanted to take the risk when it was their own child at stake, certainly not me. Montessori exercises, word cards, classical music—all were welcome in large doses. When a study—not that it showed anything my mother friends and I didn't already intrinsically know—turned up that London cabbies, who take years to learn the city's routes, have experienced brain growth in the hippocampus, not much attention was paid. (When interviewed, one of the cabbies said, *I never noticed part of my brain growing—it makes you wonder what happened to the rest of it.*) I knew a good opportunity to enslave myself when I saw one. Gabriel had to be saved, and it was up to me to do the saving, and so I waded, dragging R along with me, through therapies and books and workshops, and ticked through activity lists for each area of development—speech, gross motor, fine motor—that I tacked up on the fridge. R was somewhat more lighthearted, and the term *gross motor* made him laugh his guts out.

All of this bears little resemblance to the developmental notions that existed when I was little (and which probably accounts for my embrace of the later one), which, coming only a couple of decades after the lobotomy was thought a viable response to psychosis, seemed to concentrate on rectifying physical aberrations like curving spines and club feet with restraints that only a dominatrix could love, and leaving the brain to its mysteries. One of my sisters had muscle tone so low that she didn't walk until well into toddlerhood and, according to the evidence, had to be propped up with pillows for photographs. There wasn't a physical therapist in sight, and likely no such thing where we lived, only the family musings later on. Similarly, when I developed a stutter at age four, there were no speech pathologists and forms to fill, and the stutter vanished by age six, another family legend about the uncanniness of child development.

We were nearing the end of the paperwork when the social worker asked, *What age do you think he is developmentally?* As long as I've been asked it, I've found this a difficult question, largely because it wants to render experience irrelevant. It's a question that suggests, for instance, that a forty-year-old woman with minimal language, difficulty relating to others, and a doll tucked under her arm, but who also holds a job, has been to Paris with her sister, and, let's not forget, has experienced the opening and closing of day and night for forty years, is the same as an eight-year old. I told the social worker that it was impossible to say. I couldn't answer it.

She asked me again, as if she hadn't heard me.

I don't really know, I told her. We went back and forth. She appeared unflustered, though curious. She pressed forward, spurred on by the twinkling blank on her assessment, and it seemed to me impossible to place him there. He could fit, on the other hand, inside the complicated rooms of jazz, where he could tolerate a spectrum of sound that many adults found difficult to bear. He'd had to endure seizures, and countless strangers' stares, and learn the interior of waiting, the gray space of the outsider. He'd had to wear spectacles, have his tonsils out and tubes put in his ears. He'd had pneumonia and been in a hospital's isolation ward during a meningitis scare. He was master to a thousand storms and hurricanes, and helpless to another thousand. He'd traveled over borders, on oceans, and in skies (a homeless woman in Bermuda would grab his hands and cry, *I feel the heat off him—I feel the heat!*). He loved his peanut butter and jam sandwiches, and also Thai and Indian food. He'd watched his words go. He'd spent time in the hot cell of inarticulate longing, or rage, or sadness, without the key of words. Imagine when he wakes and remembers his life, how his freedoms are small and nuanced and his boundaries so heavily guarded. You have to imagine, also, the inverse of this, since every tension has an opposing one. You have to imagine a joy in him so profound that boundaries fall away. You have to imagine acceptance.

So the difficulty, then, as this woman was patiently waiting for me to say something she could write down, something other than *I don't know*, was stuffing his experience into the notion of a toddler. I took the toddler's primal edginess, the snuffling prickliness, and laid it against the Gabriel I knew, and I could see qualitatively, they were not the same.

But the void has a way of drawing toward it anything that hasn't been nailed down. It wasn't her fault. I liked her, and she was, as they say, just doing her job. It was very possible that she hated asking the question as much as I hated answering it. There was Dr. P, in his speech right after his son died: . . . *there is a goodness, kindheartedness, humanity, and magic in our children that must be protected and never be betrayed.*

But with very little words, I betrayed both Gabriel and me. Little words.

He's two, I said to the woman holding her black pen to the white space on the page.

✳

When he turns eleven, we have a party at a café where we go to hear jazz. Thirty of his school friends come, and some of the parents stay, too, because the music is swinging. There is a sax player and a drummer, both family friends, and they play while the kids, and Gabriel too in his own way, dance wildly. When the cake comes, loaded with candles, the lights are dimmed and the sax and drums get going on a wild, looping version of the birthday song with thirty singing kids, and I can't help but think how when Gabriel was born, he should have been met with a celebration. But none of us were ready, least of all him.

I don't know the recipe for making yourself ready. Like the guys joining Miles Davis in 1959 for the recording of the album *Kind of Blue*, you get a set of suggestions and you're just told to play. You should know how by now, right? One morning before Gabriel gets ready for school, he and I sit on his bedroom floor, listening to "Flamenco Sketches" on his stereo. He sits on the hardwood in his pajamas, and I sit facing him. "Flamenco Sketches" began in the studio with Davis as a bunch of note suggestions by Bill Evans: *Play in the sound of these scales.* That was all. Davis, Coltrane, Adderley, Chambers, Cobb, Evans, they were all ready, ready to take a loose guide like that and make something of it. Something iconic. Something that a boy who doesn't talk can fit inside. I don't know how many times I've heard the tune before, it would be many, but I don't know that I have ever really listened, or listened in the way that Gabriel is listening. He opens a door for me, and I step inside. Is this what it's like to be him? Or what it's like to be him at least some of the time? I am never ready, I am never ready. I am ready.

figment [no.3]

I am finishing my run on a paved trail that leads away from a refurbished train station and there he is, a big brown-and-white boxer, bounding along, stopping and waiting, wanting to play, wanting something. He is like the frayed end of an electrical charge. When I started out, two teenage girls were walking a pair of whippets, slight as needles, matchsticks. Weaving behind them was the boxer. I assumed at first that he belonged to them also, but it became apparent that they were trying to shield their dogs from him. Later on, two men asked if I was missing a dog, and there was something premonitory about this; he was already attached to me, invoked as missing.

Being untethered means coming apart. He halts when he sees me. I pass him at a slower pace, then hear him galloping on the pavement behind me, feel the buzz of instinct brighten and burst. I wheel around with my hand up, *Stop!* And he stops.

Maybe there's something about being fatigued to which neediness is anathema. I want to flee his size, his strangeness, and what seems like his predicament. He is nothing if not coming apart. I wasn't always like this, strung out and unwilling to help a poor dog, but there he is, lost, in need—and I can't abide it. That and the dirty bandage on his ear.

I turn and walk this time, afraid that if I run, I'll morph into prey. He follows me again, and again I turn and yell *Stop!* And turn away from him, try to shut him out, get to my car. But we continue on this way, stopping and starting, a rhythmic push and tug as he draws me closer and I try to disentangle. I tell him for what I hope is the final time, *Go away!*, but he just plants himself on the pavement and tilts his head. He even looks like his feelings are hurt. We watch each other, and I have a moment to take in his size fully. He is dense and muscular and weighs, I think, not so much less than I do. Black eyes and erect ears, all the better to predict in me every agitated shift. Worse, though, is the loop he has drawn around me, he is so terribly lost.

Oh all right . . . Goddamn it, all right. He sits closer to my feet while I feel for the tag on his collar. I find it and then start to laugh. *Goober . . . Jesus.* He drenches my hand as I pull away. There is a phone number, and so I decide to take him to my car to call it, reach what will turn out to be his mistress. Her voice on the phone will sound frantic, and she will say how she's been looking all over for him, and then she'll speed to the train station to collect him. And he will turn and look at me before leaving so I can tell him, *It was nice to meet you.*

But for now, I head to my car and hear his nails on the pavement behind me. It occurs to me that maybe from his view I am the one who is missing. Maybe it's me who, like words and color, has wandered from one space into another, has been lost. *C'mon boy,* I say, and as I walk through the parking lot, he follows at my side, brushes his body against me.

5 a.m.

*

rescue

Sir Ernest Shackleton, in his diary, January 26th, 1915:

Waiting

Waiting

Waiting

Admiral Richard Byrd, in his diary, June 25th, 1934:

Nothing . . . Nothing.

The image of Antarctica, the one in my mind, has the clarity of a glass bead. It's not the continuous night where Byrd sits but an empty plateau, sparkling, without a trace of pack ice. We're at the center of the place, no fringe elements here. Just a single line of horizon and an upper segment of sky almost the same color as the ice. It's only an image, so it has elasticity—it could be the size of a rice grain or the actual Antarctica. There are no markers to give away what year it is or who has been here, who has not. It's hard to imagine someone suffering inside such an image. There is no impatience in it, no malevolence, famine, or traffic lights or huts. Just one idea, something like indifference. I can see, then, the source of the problem: that this is where human longing begins. We can misunderstand a place and, believing it's empty, want to fill it.

The other essential point about the image is the sun, the way it imbues the picture without being directly there. And that's what I'm waiting for, the approach of light, which will find us different from the day before. We're a different combination of molecules, or ideas, or notes. But the light when it comes will be exactly the way it has always been, unstoppable and complete. Its approach, the tiny idea of it now, feels a little like death, something like a god, like rescue. It comes and I know that it does, that it will.

I open Byrd's book to a page that S, when he was younger and wielding a blue pen, had scribbled on. Underneath the scribble (like wires and brain waves), Byrd is experiencing his sixty-first day since the one that he fell to the floor of his tunnel. He writes,

The day was coming on; it was heaving ponderously into the north, pushing back the darkness a little bit every day, firing its own gorgeous signal pots along the horizon to a man who had

little else to look for. So there was that on my side: the miraculous expansion and growth of light, the soundless prelude to the sun, which was only twenty-seven days north of me.

Gorgeous signal pots. Exactly.

＊

S will be up soon. After his long slumber, he emerges from his room, swinging his door wide open and grinning. Sometimes his introduction to the day is a little slower, and he wraps a blanket around him, curls up on the floor with the cat outside the bathroom, and will sleepily say, *Hello, Mom*, when I walk by. If I stand outside his room right now, I'll hear his deep breathing.

It is an incident involving him that calls rescue to mind. Apart from fearing the dark and snakes in his bed, he is afraid of swimming, and so, despite numerous weeks of lessons during the summer, he still hasn't learned. His ability to passively resist the lesson while giving an appearance of participating in it is astounding. No swimming teacher yet has been able to crack his code or get him to swim unassisted. His fear has to do with rescue, whether or not it comes, but I imagine it also has to do with the way a person has to struggle badly to warrant it.

One set of lessons took place at a university swimming pool that could only be found by navigating a labyrinth of unmarked corridors. At the end, surrounded by glass, were three large pools in a row like turquoise lozenges, parents towing kids and bath towels and looking disarrayed from the trek. Muffling, chlorinated air. I sat on a bench with the other parents while S walked tentatively to where the instructors, holding clipboards and ticking off names, were gathered. A woman sat beside me with a robust baby girl whom she breast-fed while cajoling her two sons toward the instructors; the boys wore turtle-shaped goggles she said they refused to shower without.

The classes were small, and two of them were being conducted at the same time. Foam noodles were brought out for S's class, but the kids clung hard to the pool's tile edge. It seemed they all had a refined fear of wetting their faces, and their first instruction, to dip their faces in the water, provoked grimaces. S held the tile rim with one hand and brought the other to his lips, which were already turning blue.

There was a kind of suspension, or held breath, while we parents sat and watched. Swimming, once a person knows how, seems so natural that it's easy to forget the reality of that glossy, unstable surface, how the body is expected to float through it and under it. I don't remember much about learning to swim, only that I swam among jellyfish and crabs in the ocean off Prince Edward Island without care, something I couldn't do so easily now. It occurred to me while watching S's lesson how difficult it can be to do what is natural and elemental, even primal, once fear has moved in. It seems a simple enough instruction: return, partly anyway, to that calm wise being you once were. *Become* something that floats instead of sinks. Regress, basically, to when all the world was dark and you didn't mind.

The lessons had been under way for ten minutes when a boy in the preschoolers' class went under and didn't come up. He went under and didn't come up and none of us, not even the lifeguard, seemed to notice his struggle. The pool was shallow, with three small platforms for the preschoolers to stand on; he had stepped off and into a gap between two of the platforms while the instructor, helping another child paddle to the ladder, faced the other way.

Something about the number of adults and the presence of the lifeguard and life preservers, and the shallow depth of the pool itself was obscuring. We could see the boy's hands thrust up through the water's surface, begging, and the agitation beneath. He was becoming a blur, being erased, and the meaning escaped us. It seemed that he was just playing, that the froth of his thrashing was really just another version of the children kicking and blowing bubbles just a few feet away; for a long moment his motions seemed to fit.

At last, attention focused on this roiling point in the pool so ferociously that screams erupted and the instructor turned around. She grabbed the boy, pulled him clawing and vibrating from the water, and held him until he gasped and bawled. Born again. His mother came to stand like a slim line at the pool's edge. Everyone watched him being consoled as he clung, dripping, to the instructor's neck. Within moments, everything seemed to right itself, and no one said anything about it. There was not a word, just a few hard looks, and the mother receded. The lessons continued, and S's class turned back to dipping their faces.

In order for rescue to come for you, not only will you have to struggle but someone has to notice you doing so. And when rescue comes, it is often in a single movement bound by a beginning and an end—I have wondered what happens when the rescue, as in Gabriel's case, has to be sustained. Perhaps the rescue becomes something else, or assumes a subtlety it can perpetuate. Perhaps Gabriel doesn't need me to save him in the larger sense, or perhaps the many smaller, nuanced rescues taken together point to something else. Perhaps, as when he stripped his mattress and gathered his twirlies to face him, what he wants is someone to bear witness. Someone to see him. And there is this, too: by keeping me out of the shallows, Gabriel is the one who has saved me.

As for rescue, in the end both it and the struggle can be so slick that they slide from the hands; they can seem not to exist. The mother receded. And if you ask S about the boy in the water, he will say that he doesn't remember him.

The Ice

The crackling voice in the receiver tells Byrd that the journey has begun. Poulter has devised a searchlight using scrap metal; the men, five of them in a tractor, are coming as soon as the weather clears. Excitement gives way to anxiety. Byrd vomits his hot milk and cereal as the temperature on the Barrier is falling. He climbs the ladder to look north, knowing no one could be there. Even as he feels hopeless, he can feel them coming over the Barrier, as deliberate as the sun but without the elegance, staggering forward at one to two miles per hour. And the Barrier, acquiescing, allows them through a few feet at a time.

Or so he believes, hauling himself up his ladder with a tin of gasoline to set on fire. But the horizon is empty, and the lights he sometimes sees are just the stars. He returns to his hut, haunts it like a frantic, fluttering, expiring moth.

He sends inarticulate messages, sometimes shooting them blindly into the night. Cranking the transmitter exhausts him, and he wants to smash the radio. The temperature touches down at minus 80° F, and the bottle of boric acid that he uses to rinse his eyes shatters. When he goes topside, the Barrier snatches his breath and temporarily blinds him. His sleeping bag contains a pillow of ice.

The first attempt doesn't take. The Barrier wins, and the men return to Little America. Poulter reduces his team to three, including himself, and starts off again a few days later. Byrd, sifting the instrument data, decides that a hurricane is coming. But with his hut's disarray, the frozen vomit and the tumbled books, it appears that he is the storm. Eventually there is word that the men have been confounded on the crevasses, were unable to navigate around them, attempt number two is aborted, and they have turned back once again.

Murphy's voice is in the hut, asking him—directly—if he's ill, if he's hurt.

Byrd's code: *Nothing to worry about, only please don't ask me to crank anymore.*

provisions

Rescue, if it comes at all, can act like a cat ducking its head at the door of a storm. It is fallible and sometimes inconstant and relies on the one being rescued. The process is sometimes passive, and rescue is received the same way as force but interacts with its object through something like a conversation, or perhaps what is more akin to a balancing, like osmosis. It settles in one place and then moves, sometimes slowly, to another; gathers you in—if you say so—and moves you with it.

On the last morning of the year, Gabriel is finally asleep and I've gotten up for the day. A coffee mug is in my hand, and the cat is curled on my lap as I sit at my computer. A rescue is about to happen, except too late. At 6:30 a.m., the world is still dim and a man dies, perhaps a hundred yards from my house, on a road that runs perpendicular to mine.

What alerts me is the number of cars that are suddenly streaming by the house, and I become curious enough to put on my coat and head down the street to the corner. A police officer is conducting the oncoming traffic with a black-gloved hand, diverting it down my street and away from the lone maroon car and the white tarp with a body underneath. The body is just a shape, an abstraction, but among the debris where police officers are marking with small flags is a man's black boot. Not far away, a wallet and some teeth.

The maroon car is on the other side of the road and unoccupied. Police cars and emergency vehicles are skewed in various directions, and it's easy to imagine the urgency when they arrived, the sirens and lights, the sudden braking. An urgency that somehow I managed not to hear. Only a few hours after the accident, a blizzard will come causing a tractor-trailer to jackknife and countless cars to merge with trees along the roadside, but at 6:30 a.m. there is no sign of snow and not a trace of it left from the blizzard two weeks before. Rain between then and now has washed all of it away. The white sheet on the body seems heavy, like a lid, like it contains an ultimate quiet. The cold, too, the impending ice and snow, and the stopped ambulance render another heaviness, a struck string coming to rest and another just beginning to vibrate.

The mind tries to work out what death means and how it happens. The evidence is all around, but the moment of the collision has vanished, leaving the whole thing improbable. The impact has been tucked into the day already, scuttled away, and the scene is just that: a *scene*. I try to assemble what happened with the bits lying about, but there are only a few threads leading back to that moment when a portal opened and someone, shattering, stepped through. The man, whom I will learn later was thirty-one, is, in the figurative sense at least, long gone.

The road where the body lies runs straight for ages, passes by fields that in summer are full of dahlias, corn, and blueberries, an evangelical church that looks like an auto body shop, a store that sells plants and guns, and another where you can buy figurines of wizards. It's not a road where there are many pedestrians, and so

I assume at first that the body was the maroon car's driver, having flown through the windshield. In fact, the driver has been taken from the scene already, and the body belongs to a man who was crossing the road. (When spring comes, a wooden cross, painted purple, will appear close to the spot where the man was hit, and I will see a truck parked to the side and a woman kneeling, fixing a tangle of Mylar balloons to the cross.) The police officers catalogue, and a tow truck hauls the maroon car away, and the ambulance and fire vehicles eventually pull out slowly, one by one. The road recovers seamlessly, and within a couple of hours there is no trace that anything unusual has happened, no evidence that a man gestured toward Death without knowing it and that Death had been paying attention. It seems to happen so easily, so casually. There is Byrd in the Antarctic with an almost impossible rescue inching toward him, and the fact that he's been poisoned by carbon monoxide for four months and is still managing to keep alive, and then there's this, a man simply crossing the street and flying apart as he does. And there is rescue hovering all around, efficient and orderly and, like a bad guest, arriving much too late.

The thing is it feels like a visitation, like it means something in spite of elements that appear random or casual or out of the blue, and what is left is a reminder, a prod that suggests a choice is to be made between what is dead and what is living. You are not, after all, the man under the tarp. The white sheet is not yours. Not yet. You get to turn away from the curb, in the wind, clutching your coat lapels together, and walk past the cars that are turning. You get to head back to the house where the family and the cat and the cup of coffee are waiting.

So rescue comes. Sometimes it's there all along and you have been oblivious, too absorbed in the conundrums to notice it standing at the curb, tapping its foot. Sometimes it's just that you haven't needed rescue at all. You can climb from the dark space, clutching what is inevitable and unbelievable, all on your own.

I can hear Gabriel stirring inside his room, his numerous sounds, his clicks and ticks and sighs and hums, his fingers along the skin of the door, along the other side of what separates us. I remember when night was different and not the one of broken sleep and parenting, but the one when I was young and carousing with R or with friends; night then meant a different kind of discordance, and a kind of freedom, one specific to the city. I remember seeing the streets being bathed by sanitation trucks and phantoms of steam from the storm sewers. The buses full of drunks and violinists that played in the underground tunnels when we went scurrying through. On the street corners, there were pimps with pins for eyes, and farther along, the brown humps of bodies sleeping on concrete or absorbing the hot, black breath of the subway, and there always seemed to be someone hollering to no one in particular in the acidic light. Night is another land entirely, full of suicides, heart attacks, and fevers.

Also evening primrose and jasmine blooming beneath the stars. I don't repudiate night, any version of it, or disregard what is clearly its elegance and promise, its sheer size. Sometimes I can merge with the dark and float in it, not unconscious but keenly aware of it. When I had my first miscarriage, I remember the way that opposing forces seemed to come together, two streams feeding into one: *I am so alive and death is in me.* It was the beginning of this story, the start of being born. I didn't understand the night then; now I do.

I gather my robe around me and open his door. He is sitting on the floor with his legs out in front of him, and I sit down beside him. The air is cool, but it's not so bad. I smile at him, stroke his hair, and he's calm and watching me peacefully. There: his blue, impossible eyes, his *person*. I don't often encounter people who think they are equal with him. I've even seen other people with developmental delays, no doubt defaulting to what they're used to receiving, condescend to him. He is, as poet Donald Hall wrote of old people, *permanently other*. He's so permanently other that his otherness obliterates the observer's scary self-knowledge that if any of us lives long enough, we will take on characteristics that in some form or another resemble his. We will all become cautious when walking, we will need help with spoons and bath soaps and toilets and buttons, we will no longer be certain that a pen is called a pen. We will not always look at other people as if we know them. We will not always know. The membrane between him and the rest of the world is only a fallacy, a remnant of a dislocation that never happened. He has always been like everyone else, and we are utterly like him. Perhaps the sameness and seamlessness of Being are unpalatable to some, nevertheless it is the truth. *Do you belong to a secret society?*

The piano ain't got no wrong notes.

He folds his hands around my face, cups it, and I come into view. He sees me, but I no longer need him to see me. In a way, what happens to Byrd is a related circumstance; his sense of himself disintegrates without the defining gaze of anyone but his face in the mirror. He discovers that unequivocally we need other people; I'm just not sure we need the recognition of specific individuals. That Gabriel sees me, and I don't need him to say *mama* to prove it, is certainly affirming, but when he is eclipsed, or I am, by the long shadow of his episodes, it seems to me that love is still love. The themes are too large to be altered by the small us, by the weird transience of words and autism and knowing and unknowing. We exist and that's all. At this moment, he is quiet and focused, and he sees me as if he's always seen me, as if I never disappear; I kiss his face. Like the creatures discovered in the deepest parts of the ocean, we construct a light of our own.

provisions

On Gabriel's thirteenth birthday, we're in one of those long, underground spaces that seem hooked to jazz, descending another steep set of stairs and guiding his hands along the rails. The rabbit hole, the tumbling, the dark rooted smell. The spaces that contain the unpredictable and shifting and it's all right. The support pillars are brick that's been painted a glossy black, the floor is a red carpet with a crosshatch of amber lines. The ceiling is low, a velvet curtain behind the bandstand hangs from brass rings, and light glints off the trumpets and saxes on their stands, the silver on the drum set. It's the same band that's led by the emergency-room doctor. The bass player hooks his arm around the neck of the bass so the whole thing leans against him while he thumbs through a playbook. The sax player gives Gabriel five before going to the stage. The drummer's itching to get going. They swarm casually, exchange slight nods, a few words, and they start up. "The Sidewinder," by Lee Morgan, and "Moanin'," by Bobby Timmons, "Water from an Ancient Well," by Abdullah Ibrahim, "Cape Verdean Blues," by Horace Silver, various Monk. A woman gets up from the audience to sing a few tunes with them: "My Funny Valentine," "All of Me."

When the break comes, they play "Happy Birthday" and everybody in the place sings while the waitress brings out a cake for Gabriel, chocolate with vanilla frosting and yellow swirls. In the surrounding dark, the lit cake comes to him, and in the candle's light there are the faces of a dozen of the people who love him best, including four who have worked with him, pressed him onward, stood by him, and love him so well they want to be there for this. He bounces in his seat and makes one of his short, happy shrieks. R has to blow out the candle for him, and we all wish on his behalf. Pannonica asking for the three wishes; what would they be? Whatever provisions we think he needs, he likely doesn't. He holds his secrets close, and his smile in the candlelight is enormous as he gets high fives and pats on the back. What he wants now is the cake, and the music again. "Epistrophy," "Ruby, My Dear," "Body and Soul." These small delicious things.

Rescue comes like this, one song at a time.

✳

Last autumn, R and I took the boys to a large treeless field by the ocean that attracts kite flyers. On windy, sunny days, the sky is full of nylon planes, rainbows, and sharks, with their strings pinned to the ground, and the ground is full of people looking up. On the day we went, there was a noisy wind, the straining kites, and the water sparkling so hard you couldn't look at it for long. One thing we've gotten good at is finding the sun when it hovers just so. R and S launched a butterfly kite that looked like stained glass, and Gabriel and I kicked a soccer ball back and forth. Maybe because of the way the light was and how the wind filled my ears, I had one of those moments where time slows, just hangs there and then expands; we could have been there forever, I don't know. The giant butterfly grew smaller as it flew and S let out more string. Gabriel was grinning and laughing as he loped to the ball and kicked it. He was another beam of light in a moment that was like a diamond. He smiled and smiled and waited for me to return the ball, and he was unbelievably beautiful.

The Ice

The Barrier is unable, in the end, to make Byrd's hut a coffin because three men arrive from the north and save him. But you knew that. Rescue needs an accomplice: the one rescued asks, finally, for just the thing he thought he didn't need. Rescue comes to Byrd because, in code, behind the gestures of concern for his men, he pleads for it. People and light. Both, though they are known to take their sweet time, are inexorable when called upon.

He realizes when the men make their third attempt that he can assist them by making light signals from the hut that will be visible for many miles and guide the men in. He has a large kite that he's been waiting to use, one with a paper tail he can set alight so a line of fire will fly high up on the end of the string. He gathers a dozen tins of gasoline and some magnesium flares with the kite and regards the lot. He considers it his last stand.

✳

He wakes with a start, knowing that Poulter, Demas, and Waite are coming for him (of course, one of them is named Waite). Shortly after 7:30 a.m., he hauls his kite topside, soaks the tail with gasoline, and stands the kite up in the snow before lighting the tail. He isn't able to run, so he jerks the kite and it flies up to sit in the night sky, the tail blazing for what he estimates is five minutes. He will later write, *It was my first creative act in a long time.* He lights two cans of gasoline. He's exhausted and sits in the snow. The night sky is quiet, there's no response from the men, and he estimates he has about four hours before he has to do it all again.

Later afternoon, and Murphy's voice is telling him that Poulter is then ninety-three miles south of Little America and will reach him in approximately eight hours. Byrd collects his thoughts, which are racing. *It was like knowing in advance that you would be reborn again, without the intermediate obliteration of death.*

At 5:00 p.m., he sets off a gasoline can.

He tries to read *Java Head* and can't concentrate.

At 6:00 p.m., he sees something on the horizon, a light beam that rises and falls, scoring the dark, before it goes out.

He sends up another kite with a fiery tail and watches it until it dies. Then sits in the snow for half an hour, just sits. Imagine him there, folded on the snow, a little like a child, like Gabriel; the waiting. How time must close for him, a black hole with a remembered trace of searching light. How he must want to say, if only he could form the words, *I am here.*

I am still here.

He lights a gasoline can, a flare, another can. Nothing in response. He crawls inside his hut and briefly hears Murphy before he lets his earphones fall away. He sleeps for an hour and a half, and when he wakes, decides that he needs stimulants. The instructions on the bottle of strychnine say to mix one teaspoon with a glass of water; he puts three teaspoons in a cup of strong tea and drinks it down.

Another flare, which rages and dies, and then Byrd can see, sweeping over the night, the beam of Poulter's searchlight. And more than that, a second, stronger beam that he figures is a headlight.

He is close to collapse, and rescue is coming for him, but in the logic of his situation, it occurs to him that what he should do is prepare supper for the men. He heats canned soup on his stove, and returns topside to see the beam, stronger this time. Sitting in the snow, he can hear, though they are still an hour away, the horn of the tractor beeping. When I read this, I want to stop, stop everything. The Barrier has a new noise. I can almost hear the *beepbeep*, and the pounding of the heart that hears it, too.

*

No one comes for us in a tractor, sweeping a beam of light along the horizon to find our location; no one rumbles in. There are no sirens or voices carried on the Barrier to mark the silence and make it go. But rescue does come, in a way, in the form of two words.

Stop struggling. At some point, which is now lost, those are the words that arrive. Sharp and unattached to anything. A transmission, suspended in static.

The moment that I understood that Gabriel's desire to push over the lamp was something he was doing not to get a reaction out of us but because the impulse was overwhelming him was the moment that I received a lesson in relinquishing. Except that I didn't get it, not fully. It was one lesson of many. It's a daily practice to meet the oncoming force by calmly stepping aside. It makes me think of S's tantrum and the way his brain suddenly overrode his rage, allowing him to go limp on the floor so he could do the one necessary thing, which was breathe.

Stop struggling. Two years of waking to reach a phrase that seems absurdly insufficient. There is only its quiet construction: sibilant, abrupt. It calls to mind the Chinese finger puzzle that strangles the fingers more when they struggle apart.

But here is the problem, of course: how to stop an attachment to what is familiar. The struggle is interesting and vivid enough that it has become its own entity, as though it's grown a vascular system and a brain. The struggle is ruggedly handsome, and I can be myself in its arms. It doesn't expect me to be dolled up or remotely presentable. It expects my sniveling, weakened self. Yes, it's possible to say, the struggle loves me. And it's possible to be attached to its place in the hierarchy because a struggle confers importance. Sisyphus, before his rock, was the king of Corinth, after all. I have been attached to his, and Gabriel's, cycles, the close, dark space. His reliability and maybe what I perceive to be his nobility, a kind of power. He wouldn't have pissed off the gods if he weren't important to them. He stole their secrets, so says Camus. I think of Gabriel this way, as someone who holds secrets, but I don't think he stole them; he was born with them. At any rate, the mountain, the rock, the eternity, all of it a kind of power. Sisyphus accepts his fate, he stops struggling, and Camus calls him happy.

I probably don't need to tell you that when the moment comes, it's almost midnight, that time of transformations, the culmination of spells. Byrd sets off a flare and a can of gasoline, and when they finish burning, he sees the tractor with his men, stopping about a hundred yards away. He can't move toward them, so he just stands and watches them, the three men in furs coming for him. They come for him. He remembers shaking hands; it is Waite who will say later that Byrd invited them to come inside and eat soup.

> *The truth is that I could find no words to transport outward what was really in my heart. It is also said that I collapsed at the foot of the ladder. I have only a muddled impression of that and a slightly clearer one of trying to hide my weakness. Nevertheless, I do remember sitting on the bunk, watching Poulter and Demas and Waite gulp down the soup and the biscuits; and I do remember what their voices were like, even if I am not sure of what they said. And I do remember thinking that much of what they said was as meaningless as if it were spoken in an unfamiliar tongue; for they had been together a long time, occupied with common experiences, and in their talk they could take a good deal for granted. I was the stranger.*

*

Words again on the Barrier, but they can't be reclaimed. They're only words, after all, and soon enough Byrd becomes himself again, takes his place with other people. Poulter, Demas, and Waite nurse him back to health, and two months later, he is flown back to Little America. He slowly resumes command of his men and finishes the expedition, eventually pouring the whole circus into the *Bear* and the *Ruppert*, and setting sail in early February 1935, for Washington Naval Yard. (The reintroduction to the usual world happens in stages but nevertheless happens and, once on the *Ruppert*, he is entranced by a fly that he finds in his cabin.) The Depression is in its prime and so there isn't a tickertape parade to greet him, but there is a crowd and President Roosevelt. By this time, Byrd is so much a part of the world again that when one of his young daughters rushes to hug the father she hasn't seen in three years, he tells her, *Not here, dear. Later, when we're alone.*

Later, when we're alone. He has already forgotten. Rescue, after all, isn't perfect. Rescue comes only to find that you are different, and entirely the same. Maybe you are weaker, or maybe you are better. You no longer believe that rescue is for maidens and stray animals. You thought, didn't you, that a person shouldn't need rescuing, that someone in a fix should find the fix, should find the way off the Barrier, or out of the night, or away from the ledge.

Morning is coming. The light. The shapes in the dark begin to make sense. We'll play some jazz and find a spot where we fit easily, without effort. Gabriel hasn't decided against one form of jazz or another; he doesn't discount Dixieland or swing. He makes no arguments about the supremacy of bebop to cool, modal to chords, quintets to sextets, blues to fusion. He takes it all. Every story told is a story to him, and if it's told in jazz or one of its iterations, he can find his way in. I think that that is what I wish most for him, the item I would place at the top of the list of provisions. Effortlessness. Easiness.

Ease.

Tomorrow night we'll do this all over again, at least for a while. But it won't always be this way. Shift and change are positive mechanisms, too—eventually Gabriel will begin to sleep again. He'll stop shrieking. Time and wonderful teachers will be the antidotes. He'll grow older. He'll grow.

Tomorrow when midnight comes again, and night opens, there'll be Byrd and Monk and all the others, and silence, too. Possibly, there is gratitude, also, for the small hours when we are all of us alive.

Begin again.

Go back to when Gabriel was born, that hot day in June. The big clocks on the walls, and the zeppelins. He arrived lit as lightning. There was the doctor, already planning an escape, and there was me, hoping for one. There were the nurses, readying themselves, about to race, but not just yet. Gabriel, with his eyes squeezed shut, lay on my chest. Every surface was sharp.

Perhaps you didn't know this was a love story. (I think I said that Gabriel's birth was philosophically complex. Perhaps, after all, it wasn't.)

R, joyful, stood at the side of the hospital bed and clasped his hands together. *Oh, he's wonderful,* he said. *He's so wonderful.*

And I know Gabriel heard him.

The following is a list of items contained in the single sleeping berth of one of Byrd's men back at Little America and was published in the expedition's newspaper called *The Barrier Bull*. This list appeared in issue #4, 1934 (the bunk's owner is unnamed):

ALL IN ONE BUNK

2 pairs scissors, 2 pairs wristers, 3 pairs gloves, 1 steel clamp, 9 wet electric cells, 1 roll lamp wick, 1 glass of grease, 1 bottle Mistol, 1 bottle Worcestershire sauce, 1 box machine screws, 2 boxes Meta, 6 packs cards,

73 boxes matches, 1 oil can full of canvas mukluks, 6 pairs miscellaneous boots, 1 bag sennegrass, 3 rolls cotton cloth, 1 snowshoe, 8 flashlight batteries, 1 chisel, 1 pair crampons, 2 rolls plaster,

2 large jars cold cream, 3 spools thread, 1 box gum, 1 foreign soap box, 4 B batteries, 1 tube carron oil, 1 box kodak plates, 1 magneto, 1 box deodorant powder, 2 lenses, 1 large spool safety wire, 8 copies Physical Culture, 5 library books,

63 pictures of women posted on wall, 1 large box BAE I pictures, 1 package Telephone Bond, 21 rubber bands, 1 roll old photo film, 1 sheet brass 6x12, 1 electric booster,

15 feet strung wire, 3 blankets, 2 flashlights, 8 pairs holey socks, 1 pair fur liners, 8 feet Ford duraluminum, 1 tube ski wax, 1 electric magnetic light, 1 pair pliers,

1 bottle mouth wash, 2 envelopes 18x27 inches, 1 pair
stocking boards, 1 piece bread and butter,

3 tubes toothpaste, 2 blotter pads, 1 book <u>Suspicious</u>
<u>Characters</u>, 750 sheets typewriter paper, 1 oily rag, 1 spark
plug, 1 set picket wrenches, 2 carburetor valves,

1 large Stillson wrench, 1 electric plug, 1 Yale key,
1 carpenter's square, 1 pce Gerlock packing, 2 electric switches,
1 sneaker.

Byrd's other

Byrd had a ghostwriter, Charles Murphy, who was the CBS correspondent on the Ice with him and who helped him produce *Alone*
along with his other books. When I first read *Alone*, I was not only
interested in what Byrd was doing in the Antarctic but in the way
the account was written. I eventually came across a *Boston Globe* ar-
ticle from 1987 that mentioned Murphy's presence as ghostwriter.
I was momentarily disappointed, as some of my attachment to Byrd
centered around his ability, when not using Morse code, to communicate. However, I've come to think that, considering the loneliness
that is at the heart of the book, it's possibly appropriate that he
wasn't alone in having to put his experience on paper. Eventually
I was lucky enough to go to the Byrd Polar Research Center in
Columbus, Ohio, and get a look at some of the correspondence

between Murphy and Byrd about *Alone*. Some of it was written in a tone not so different from any other close partnership that has endured many years and hit some rough spots along the way. When Byrd was still in his hut and Murphy had been trying to convince the other men of the need to rescue him, he said *I don't pretend to know the man* (they had known each other for years). In one of his letters to Byrd (June 30, 1938), however, he wrote, . . . *I think I can describe certain aspects of your experience better than you can, and feel them almost as keenly. With what you give me, I can get inside your mind* . . . , and this latter statement is probably not so far from the truth. Certainly, I think that Murphy is responsible for making *Alone* what it is, and doubtless many of my favorite lines in it are attributable to him.

Notes on Quoted Material

vii   *There is no sun without shadow: The Myth of Sisyphus*, Albert Camus (First Vintage International Edition, 1991).

26   *The silence of this place: Exploring with Byrd*, Richard E. Byrd (G. P. Putnam's Sons, 1937).

46   provisions: The lists of provisions appearing here and between subsequent chapters are courtesy of the Byrd Polar Research Center Archival Program at Ohio State University.

53   *You know what's the loudest noise: Thelonious Monk: The Life and Times of an American Original*, Robin D. G. Kelley (Free Press, 2009).

61   *What I touch, what resists me: The Myth of Sisyphus*, Albert Camus (First Vintage International Edition, 1991).

76   *The body's judgment:* Ibid.

77   Pannonica de Koenigswarter: *Three Wishes: An Intimate Look at Jazz Greats*, Pannonica de Koenigswarter (Abrams Image, 2008).

85   *Radiant beams: The Music and Life of Beethoven*, Lewis Lockwood (W. W. Norton and Company, 2003).

91   huge expanses of white that surround Byrd: *The South Pole: A Historical Reader*, edited by Anthony Brandt (National Geographic Adventure Classics, 2004).

102   I think of Byrd, and also Monk: *Hear Me Talkin' to Ya: The Story of Jazz as Told by the Men Who Made It*, Nat Shapiro and Nat Hentoff (Dover, 1955); and *Thelonious Monk: The Life and Times of an American Original*, Robin D. G. Kelley (Free Press, 2009).

129   He had had a son with Down syndrome: *Honouring Christian Pueschel's Legacy*, Siegfried Pueschel, MD (*Down Syndrome News*, The Newsletter of the National Down Syndrome Congress, Vol. 23, No.7).

133   the sturdy *Endurance: Endurance: Shackleton's Incredible Voyage*, Alfred Lansing (Basic Books, 2007).

134   *I cannot write about it:* Ibid.

136   "Summertime" lyrics used by permission of Alfred Music Publishing Co. Inc. Music and lyrics by George Gershwin, DuBose and Dorothy Heyward, and Ira Gershwin. © 1935 (Renewed). All rights administered by WB MusicCorp.

Credits and Acknowledgments

Writing this book led me on an odyssey of reading about exploration, jazz, silence, and night. In particular, the stories and photographs from people who have explored Antarctica enabled me to visit that sacred place, if only figuratively. After reading Byrd's *Alone*, I moved on to his other books, *Exploring with Byrd* and *Discovery*, and to Lisle Rose's *Explorer: The Life of Richard E. Byrd*, Apsley Cherry-Garrard's *The Worst Journey in the World*, Roland Huntford's *The Last Place on Earth*, Alfred Lansing's *Endurance*, and Stephen J. Pyne's *The Ice* (Pyne's book was especially helpful in pinning down Antarctica's existential nature), and many more that were extremely helpful. Other vital references were Robin D. G. Kelley's *The Life and Times of Thelonious Monk: An American Original*, Ted Gioia's *The History of Jazz*, Barry Cooper's *Beethoven*, and Steven Naifeh and Gregory White Smith's *Van Gogh: The Life*.

Thank you to Laura Kissel, curator of the Archival Program at the Byrd Polar Research Center at Ohio State University, who was so enormously helpful and provided access to Byrd's letters, notebooks, and photographs.

Unending thanks go to my agent, Nathaniel Jacks, for being *Know the Night*'s champion and the kind of astute reader and friend that writers dream of finding. I have many editorial staff to thank: Louise Dennys and Leah Miller, who gave an enormous amount of feedback and strength to the book; Amanda Betts, Millicent Bennett, and Sarah Nalle. Thank you to Anne Collins. Other responders and encouragers along the way: Mary Cappello, Patricia Magosse, Matthew Shaer.

Small sections of *Know the Night* have appeared, in different form, in the following journals: *Ocean State Review*, *Bayou Magazine*, and *Literary Mama*. Thank you to them for their support.

Thank you also: Hope Penny, Sharon Schubert, Jean Leich and family, Denise Braum, and Jill Lieberman; the Mutch and Wilson families; and the many teachers, aides, and therapists who have helped Gabriel and his family so spectacularly for so many years, especially the staff of Stony Lane Elementary, where he enjoyed the many benefits of full inclusion; Davisville Middle School; and the Pathways Program at the Trudeau Center, all in Rhode Island.

Gratitude to the jazz musicians who made our nights hop and jump: Doug Woolverton, John Monllos, Art Manchester, Barry Lieberman, Jesse-Ray Leich, Frank Bronchicine, the Dan Hartman Quintet, and so many others.

Most especially, to my husband, Robin, and my sons, Gabriel and Samuel, the absolute lights and loves of my life:

You must imagine a gratitude more profound than *thank you* can convey.

About the Author

Maria Mutch was born in Nova Scotia and studied visual art at York University in Toronto. Her poems and essays have appeared in various literary journals, and her short story "Hot Hot Day" received a citation from the Canadian National Magazine Awards. She currently lives with her husband and two boys in Rhode Island. *Know the Night* is her first book.